BIG MONEY

BIG MONEY

What It Is, How We Use It, and Why Our Choices Matter

REBECCA DONNELLY

HENRY HOLT AND COMPANY

NEW YORK

Henry Holt and Company, *Publishers since 1866*
Henry Holt® is a registered trademark of Macmillan Publishing Group, LLC
120 Broadway, New York, NY 10271 • mackids.com

Text copyright © 2023 by Rebecca Donnelly.
Illustrations copyright © 2023 by Jen Keenan.
All rights reserved.

Our books may be purchased in bulk for promotional, educational, or business use. Please contact your local bookseller or the Macmillan Corporate and Premium Sales Department at (800) 221-7945 ext. 5442 or by email at MacmillanSpecialMarkets@macmillan.com.

Library of Congress Cataloging-in-Publication Data is available.

First edition, 2023
Book design by Mallory Grigg and Abby Granata
Printed in the United States of America by
Lakeside Book Company, Harrisonburg, Virginia.

ISBN 978-1-250-85313-4 (hardcover)
1 3 5 7 9 10 8 6 4 2

For Sandhya

Introduction

It's another day on the farm. Your job is to clean the dragon coop and check on the dragon eggs. It's taking forever for them to hatch, and you have to start your homework in half an hour. You could speed it up: Fast hatching costs 1,000 pieces of gold. You've saved 4,000 pieces, but you'll need 3,500 for a new, bigger dragon coop for all the babies.

You've probably guessed that we're in a video game world where your virtual gold can buy goods, like dragon coops, and services, like faster hatching time.

Video games let you make choices about earning, spending, and saving when you play. The study of those choices is called *economics*, and the ideas of economics apply in virtual worlds just like in real life.

Economics isn't only about the type of money we spend, whether it's virtual gold or real dollars. It's about how we use resources, like water, oil, and steel. It's about how the government decides to spend the money we pay in taxes and the decisions businesses make to earn a profit. It's about choices. Deciding how much time to spend playing your video game and how much time to spend on your homework is economics, too.

As we'll see, economics is also about well-being, ours and the planet's. How can a decision about hatching dragon eggs in a virtual fantasy world make a real person's life better—or worse?

We'll find some answers to that question and others as we look at how economics—what we decide to do with our money, our time, and our resources—connects us, from video games to our global community.

CHAPTER ONE

What Is Money?

Eight-ton limestone discs. Digital code. Wooden rectangles with pictures of pooping donkeys. What do these things have in common?

They've all been used as currency somewhere in the world at some point. A group of people decided that the stones, the code, and the pooping donkeys had value, and they would accept them in exchange for goods and services. All you need in order to have a currency is an object and a shared idea of what it should be worth. And, of course, you need people to use it.

Money and currency are related, but they're not exactly the same thing. *Money* is the unit we use to measure value, and *currency* is the physical, touchable, "real" thing that we can spend. In the United States, we measure value in dollars (that's our money), and we can spend dollar bills and twenty-five-cent coins (that's our currency). Because it's much more common to use the word "money" for both of those things, that's what we'll mostly do here.

But where did the idea of money come from? Money seems so normal in twenty-first-century America, it's even kind of weird to ask what it is. It's money! We spend it on stuff, and then we try to get more of it.

But it's not really that simple. Physical money hasn't always existed, not as coins or paper or even donkey pics. So, without money, how did people get the stuff they needed?

TRADE YOU?

Maybe you've heard that pre-industrial societies used bartering instead of money. Bartering is a direct trade of one thing for another. The story of bartering goes like this: Say that your cow made extra milk, so you made some cheese. You want to make a cheese omelet, but you don't have any eggs. How do you get them? You barter: You find someone with eggs, and together you decide a fair trade of eggs and cheese.

The problem with bartering like this is that you have to find someone who has what you need and needs what you have at exactly the time that you need what they have. But what if no one wants your cheese? Do you push a huge wheel of cheese around your village, hoping someone will find it attractive? What if it goes bad before you find someone to trade with? If direct trade was the only way to get stuff, a lot of people would be out of luck.

So, the story says, the government steps in to fix the problem. It invents a system that substitutes a token of some kind, maybe metal or stone, so that no one has to carry cheese in their pockets when they go shopping. Everyone can trade tokens instead. Voilà, money!

The problem is that this story is most likely wrong.[1] People did trade for things, but we don't know of any society that used this type of one-thing-for-another exchange system to run an entire economy. Bartering did exist in the ancient world and still does in some places, but it was never the main way people did business, and it didn't lead to the invention of money. In fact, bartering happened often in places where people already used money, but the currency itself was hard to get.

Many ancient records of business deals show that while people traded in goods, they usually thought of value in terms of something like money. For example, in Egypt, a seller would offer a copper pot at the marketplace, saying it was worth a certain amount of silver.[2] The buyer might offer barley or cloth in exchange, but the seller only accepted the trade if it was worth the same amount of silver. The difference between this kind of trade and bartering is that bartering doesn't compare goods to a measurement of value like silver or dollars.

In many societies, bartering was only used by groups that didn't know each other. You wouldn't regularly trade cheese for eggs with your neighbor because in small, close-knit communities, you didn't need to trade directly to survive. Instead, other systems of sharing usually existed. In the Haudenosaunee Confederacy in what is now the northeastern United States, each household lived on what it could hunt, gather, or grow,[3] but some goods were stored communally in longhouses and given out by the women's council.[4]

IOU ONE!

If money didn't come from bartering, where did it come from?

Big surprise: No one is absolutely sure. We do know that systems of debts (what you owe someone) and credits (what someone owes you) were everywhere in the ancient world before money existed. This might be where our modern idea of money began.[5]

When we talk about debt today, we usually mean things like credit cards and college loans. This is a little different from the kind of debt we'll talk about next, which was a common system where everyone ended up owing small amounts to everyone else.

Imagine finding a 5,000-year-old IOU! In the temples of ancient Sumer (modern-day Iraq), clay tablets were used to write down people's debts.[6] In fact, this is the oldest type of writing anywhere in the world.

Before our world was so interconnected, many small societies had their own local economies that ran mainly on credit. English villagers, for example, measured value with pounds and pence, but they didn't always use the coins themselves.

Instead, everyone ran up credit tabs at other businesses in the community: the grocer, the saddle maker, the local pub. Everyone owed their neighbors, and everyone was owed something by their neighbors. A couple of times a year, a village reckoning would be held, and all ordinary debts and credits would be canceled out. Anything that was too large to be canceled out would be paid in coins or an equivalent amount of goods.[7]

How did a system of debt and credit turn into a system of real, physical money? It probably went something like this: Your neighbor gives you an IOU for that giant cheese wheel. Later, when you want help fixing a hole in your roof, you pay a roofer with the same IOU. Instead of owing you, your neighbor now owes the roofer. An IOU could travel around a community, and as people began to accept that these notes had value, they became currency.

COLD, HARD CASH

The earliest record of this is in Szechuan Province, China, around 1000 AD,[8] when people started trading IOUs in a similar way. Instead of spending the iron coins that were used as currency at the time, people stored the coins with a local merchant who gave them a paper receipt in return. The receipt could then be traded, just as the coins had been traded before.

Coins were used as currency long before paper money. Around 600 BC,[9] in the area that we now call Turkey, jewelers hammered small pieces of metal flat and stamped them with their special mark. These are the oldest coins we know of.

The value of coins was usually based on the type of metal they were made of. Gold, silver, bronze, and iron all have different values based on how rare they are and what characteristics they have. For example, gold doesn't rust, so gold is a good choice for jewelry, and it's considered more valuable than iron. This is partly why people

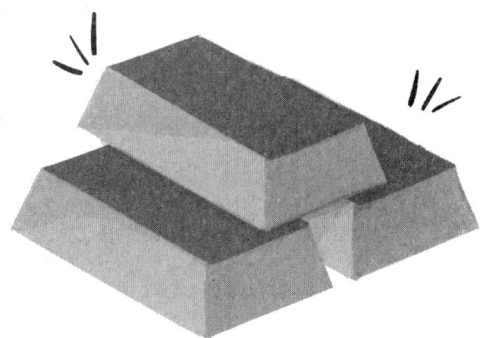

in Szechuan embraced paper money: It wasn't practical to haul around enough iron coins to spend because they weren't worth much. A pound of salt cost a pound and a half of iron coins![10]

As we started doing most of our business with strangers instead of with people we knew, having a trustworthy currency became much more important. Official money made it harder to cheat or trick people. Have you heard the phrase *Money is the root of all evil*? It's been said that in fact, evil is the root of all money![11]

REALLY BIG MONEY

But money isn't all about business and trade. Let's take a look at another of the currencies we mentioned at the beginning of this chapter.

Yap, an island in Micronesia, has two kinds of money: dollars for everyday use and rai, or stone money carved into circles, for ceremonial use. Today, you'd buy everyday things with dollars, but rai might be used as gifts for birth or marriage. In the past, rai could be used for buying everything from food to paying a war debt.[12] This isn't as rare as it sounds: The history of economics has a lot to do with war and slavery, which are unfortunately two of the oldest human activities.

Rai were quarried on Palau, an island almost 300 miles away. Some rai are small enough to hold, but the ones that made Yap famous are several feet wide, some as tall as a person. If they needed to be moved, a long pole would be put through a hole carved in the center, and two people would hoist the pole onto their shoulders.

Once a rai was brought somewhere, it didn't move often. Traditionally, families might keep their rai outside their homes to show their worth. Today, they are often seen

outside hotels or in the village bank, an outdoor collection of massive stones set up in a public space.[13]

Large rai could be exchanged without actually being moved. In fact, one fell from the boat on its journey from the quarry, but it continues to be traded today, even though it's still sitting on the ocean floor![14]

If it sounds unusual to own money without ever actually having it in your possession, it's not too different from how anyone with a bank account handles most of their earning and spending today. When you pay for something with a debit card or a pay app, your money might as well be invisible. You're just changing a few lines of digital code, subtracting a number from your bank account and adding it to the store's account.

You might think that the largest rai would be more valuable than smaller rai, but that's not necessarily true. Each rai has its own story, passed down from the generations before, which determines how much it's worth.

The oldest rai were quarried and carved using shell and stone tools and brought back to Yap in small boats. Later, Europeans came to the island, introduced iron tools, and brought rai back to Yap on their large ships.

Iron tools and large boats made the process easier, which made those rai less valuable. Today, even small traditionally carved rai can be worth more than larger ones that were quarried with European tools. The value of any individual rai comes from Yapese history and culture itself.

INVISIBLE MONEY

As we've seen, the invention of money is partly about making trade easier. Coins in the ancient world had all the properties that are still useful in currency today: They were long-lasting and easy to carry (at least in small quantities), and they could be used to measure value and to pay for things.

They had another important characteristic, too: scarcity. When something is rare and in demand, its value rises. Even paper money is rare, not because paper is hard to find but because governments decide how much paper money to print. If we used homemade Unicorn Dollars or chunks of gravel instead of coins, we would have no way to control the amount of money in the system, so its value would be very low.

We pointed out that most transactions these days are done with invisible money, which exists in computer code. But did you know that banks can actually use this process to create money? Every time a bank makes a loan, it's making brand-new money!

This might be one of the hardest things to understand about how money works. It's easy to think about money when it's a fixed amount in your wallet. It's a lot harder to think about it as something that can be created out of nowhere. Making loans helps the economy grow, and as long as the loans get repaid, the system works the way it's supposed to.

But how much physical cash is actually out there? In 2021, there was about $2.07 trillion in circulation[15] (currency moving around between

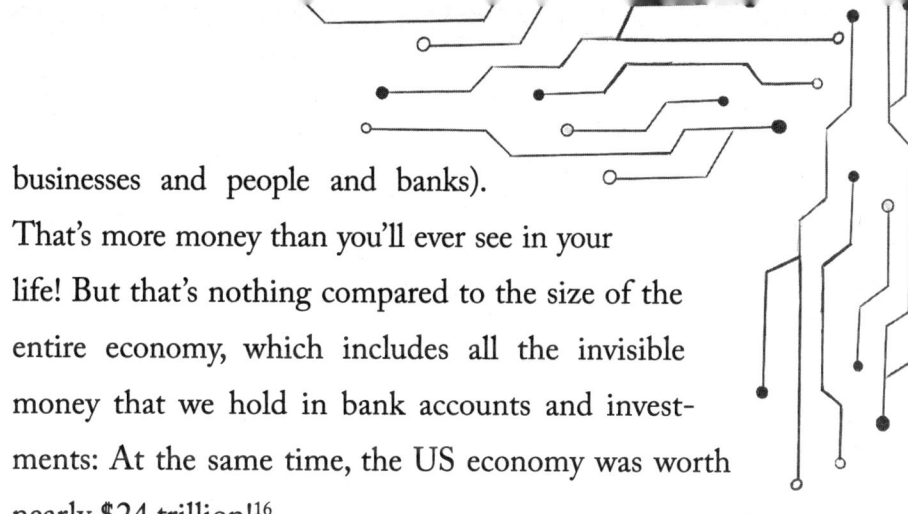

businesses and people and banks). That's more money than you'll ever see in your life! But that's nothing compared to the size of the entire economy, which includes all the invisible money that we hold in bank accounts and investments: At the same time, the US economy was worth nearly $24 trillion![16]

BLOCKED

Recently, another kind of invisible money has been getting a lot of attention: *cryptocurrency*. Cryptocurrency, or crypto, is a type of virtual money that exists outside the system of banks and governments. The first cryptocurrency, bitcoin, was created in 2008 after a huge financial crisis in which many people lost their jobs and homes[17] and trust in banks was low. The idea behind it was to use digital technology to create an independent, fair financial system.

Here's how it works: Bitcoin and other cryptocurrencies are created and stored on a decentralized network called a *blockchain*. This means that no single organization is responsible for controlling its value or recording transactions. Instead, every transaction is recorded on the blockchain:

Every computer in the network records every transaction at once. This is supposed to make bitcoin more trustworthy, sort of like making a promise in front of your entire class. But there's a downside to having this kind of independent system: Because no one is overseeing it, you can lose access to your crypto wallet if you forget your password.

Crypto scams are big business, too. In 2018, the CEO of a cryptocurrency exchange (a marketplace for buying and selling cryptocurrencies) died, and the passcode to his encrypted computer died with him. Over 100,000 people lost access to their accounts. Later on, an investigation discovered that the company had been scamming its customers even before the CEO's death, moving hundreds of millions of dollars off the blockchain and into its own private accounts.[18]

At the moment, cryptocurrencies are popular investments, but they aren't often used to buy things. El Salvador was the first country to make bitcoin a legal currency,[19] but in most other countries, you can't spend it easily. The first transaction to use bitcoin happened in 2010, when a man in Florida bought two pizzas for 10,000 bitcoin, or $25.[20] That probably wouldn't work at your local pizza place.

Bitcoin's price has changed a lot since then. In November 2021, one bitcoin was worth $69,000. In November 2022, its value was down to $21,000.[21] But how can something that was created out of nothing have any value? It's partly scarcity: There will only ever be 21 million bitcoin in existence.

It also takes a lot of electricity to mine, or earn, bitcoin. Computers earn bitcoin by solving complicated math puzzles. The first computer to solve a particular puzzle wins the bitcoin, so miners compete against one another to run more, faster computers.[22] That requires power! In one year, bitcoin uses as much energy as a small country like Malaysia.[23] That doesn't count other cryptocurrencies and blockchain technologies like non-fungible tokens (NFTs), digital certificates of ownership for online artworks and other content. Energy use is a very real cost that gives bitcoin some of its value, even as it emits over 24 million tons of CO_2 every year, contributing to global warming.[24]

So far the value of bitcoin has risen and fallen so wildly that it hasn't proven to be a good way to run an economy. Most Salvadorans don't use it and most businesses don't take it, even though they're supposed to by

law. But maybe that's a good thing: A year after the government made it an official currency, bitcoin's value was down by more than half! Cryptocurrency is still such a new technology that it's hard to tell how things will look in the future. Will crypto become a useful currency or stay as it is, an investment with potentially high risks and rewards?

IN $ WE TRUST

Ultimately, every currency relies on trust. It's ironic that currency is useful to us because we can use it to do business with people we've never met and that we have no reason to trust, but our entire money system would fall apart if we didn't all trust in one important idea: that our money is worth something, whether it's made of paper or binary code.

We all use money because we all believe everyone else will accept it and use it, too. As soon as people stop believing money is worth something—poof! It's worthless. That's pretty serious magic.

What about that pooping donkey money, though?

It was used briefly in parts of Germany around the First World War. The German economy was in such bad shape that a variety of *notgeld*, or "emergency money," was printed on everything from foil to compressed coal dust to give Germans a way to pay for things. There were no computers at the time, so virtual money wasn't an option.

The donkey was only one of many types of notgeld, some issued by the government and some by local towns and even by clubs. By 1924, Germany stopped allowing people to print and use notgeld, and the pooping donkey and its friends became collectors' items, as they still are today.[25]

What happens to your currency when it's not considered money anymore? In the case of the donkey notgeld, even the people who made the currency knew it wouldn't be good forever. Below the donkey was printed as a joke about how anyone who used this money was a donkey, too.

CHAPTER TWO

How Does Money Work?

At first, this seems like another question with an obvious answer: Money works when we spend it! Right?

Say a brownie sundae costs $4.99 at your favorite ice cream parlor. You have $5—perfect! You can have a brownie sundae plus one shiny penny for your piggy bank. Isn't that all we need to know about how money works?

Not quite. Every question about money leads to more questions! For one thing, there's probably tax on that sundae, meaning you'll have to pay more than $4.99. Why? And why did you decide to buy a brownie sundae at this ice cream parlor? Did you compare prices with all the other ice cream parlors in town? How did the manager decide to charge $4.99 for a brownie sundae? What is the person behind the counter getting paid? And how did you get that $5 in the first place?

Told you there were a lot of questions.

ECONOMIC SYSTEMS

In chapter 1, we saw that money is basically an agreement between people that something has value and can be used to exchange goods and services. An economic system is the set of rules and practices that tell us *how* to use it.

Economic systems supply people with what they want and need. There are three main types of modern economic systems: *command economies*, *market economies*, and *mixed economies*. What makes them different is how much control the government has over how business gets done.

A command economy is completely controlled by the government. You might have heard another term that goes with command economies: *communism*. Communism is a political ideology that spread from Russia to about one-third of the world in the twentieth century,[26] but here we'll concentrate on its economic effects. (Remember our funny currencies in chapter 1? When communism ended in Russia in the early 1990s and the economy went through rapid changes, goods like bricks and towels were briefly more valuable than rubles, the official Russian currency—imagine getting paid in towels![27])

In a command system, all industry and trade, from factories to mines to the local bakery, are controlled by the government, or publicly owned. The government uses central planning to decide what to manufacture, what to grow, and what to sell. The government also sets prices.

In a market economy, most businesses are owned by private companies, not the government, and supply and demand are the forces that make trade work and determine what things cost. Private companies might be owned and run by a single person, a couple of people, or a group of people. Grocery stores, car manufacturers, big tech companies, and restaurants are all private businesses.

A mixed economy is what it sounds like: There's a mix of private and public business. In mixed economies, the government sets rules for how businesses can run.[28]

Strictly speaking, the United States has a mixed economy, although we usually say we have a market economy. (Confusing!) That's because there are other countries where the government has much more control over things like trains, energy supplies, and health care. But the government plays a significant role in the American economy, from public schools and colleges to tax laws and safety regulations.

No country in the world has a completely free market economy, or one with no government control. That would be almost impossible! Roads, for example, are usually public.

What if you had to pay to walk down a street? Or what if there were no rules telling companies to make sure food and medicines are safe?

One more definition. You might have heard the word *capitalism*, and you might know that it also has something to do with money and business. Where does capitalism fit in to our definitions of economic systems? It goes along with market systems and mixed economies. Capitalism is about owning "capital," which can be anything from land to factories to patents on technology. Capital is put to work to make profits for the people and companies that own it. Capitalism and the market work together.

We'll mostly talk about market economies and capitalism in this book, since that's what we have in the United States.

THIS LITTLE BROWNIE WENT TO MARKET

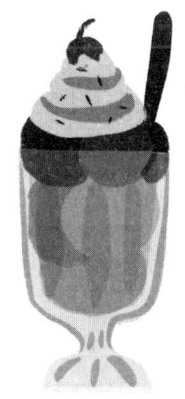

What *is* this mysterious "market"? We're not talking about supermarkets or farmers markets, although those are examples of businesses that operate in the market. The "market" just refers to all the buying, selling, producing, and consuming that happens anywhere. The market for brownie sundaes includes all the companies that make ice cream, toppings, and brownies; everyone who sells sundaes; and anyone who wants to buy a sundae.

In a market economy, anyone can start a business. As long as you follow the rules (get a business license, pay taxes, pay your employees, and follow any special rules of your industry), you can set up shop. You might also need money to buy equipment, advertise, or rent a space: As they say, you have to spend money to make money!

Imagine you wanted to open your own ice cream parlor, Brownie Sundays. You'd need to do some research and find out how many other ice cream parlors there are in town, where they're located, and what they offer. The success of Brownie Sundays will depend on how well it competes with similar businesses. Let's look at some of the things that affect businesses in the market.

SUPPLY, DEMAND, AND INVISIBLE HANDS

The goal of private companies is to make a profit, or earn more money than it costs to provide goods or services.

Prices are set by the market, which (usually) follows the

law of supply and demand. Laws in economics aren't quite like laws in hard sciences like physics. The law of gravity is always in effect, but the "law" of supply and demand can—and does—get broken regularly.

Supply depends on getting ingredients for brownie sundaes and finding workers to serve them. The number of other ice cream parlors in the area matters, too. *Demand* depends on the number of people who want brownie sundaes and have the money to buy them.

Supply and demand work together. When demand for something is high, the price will also (usually) be higher. If there's a line down the block for your brownie sundaes, you can probably charge $5.99 instead of $4.99 because you know that people want them. The other side of the law of demand is that once you raise the price, fewer people will want them, so demand will go down.[29]

The law of supply says that as the price for something rises, companies will supply more of it. If the price of a brownie sundae goes up to $5.99 and your business is more profitable, you might rent a larger space or open another shop across town. But the other side of the law of supply is that when there's more of something, the price usually goes down!

Together, supply and demand work in a way that Adam Smith, one of the founders of economics in the eighteenth century, called "the invisible hand." Demand goes up, prices rise. Companies see that prices are rising, so they increase supply, but when the supply increases, prices go down. Supply and demand ensure the efficient allocation of scarce resources, or how to get a limited amount of stuff to the people who want or need it.

If you open ten Brownie Sundays in the same neighborhood and charge $5.99 for a sundae, the supply will be too high, and there won't be enough demand for you to make a profit. The most profitable thing to do is to have one location and maybe another across town and charge about the same price as everyone else. That's the invisible hand at work!

COMPETITION, OR I'M BETTER THAN YOU

In a market system, most businesses have competition. Every other ice cream parlor is competition for Brownie Sundays. You could even consider places that sell other kinds of desserts as competition. When someone wants something sweet, they can go to a bakery, a grocery store, a corner store, a gas station, a dollar store, a café, and so on. When two or more companies sell the same or similar things, they're each other's competition.

The opposite of competition is a *monopoly*. That's when one company controls the market and the price for a product. Today, laws exist to prevent companies from forming monopolies, but some parts of the economy are under what's called a natural monopoly. The gas supply that many of us use for heating and cooking is a good example. It doesn't make sense for different companies to start putting in their own gas lines to compete with each other.

Sundae-Mart decides to offer a $4.47 brownie sundae. In the perfectly rational world of economics, this would cause every other ice cream parlor to start selling their brownie sundaes for $4.47. If one business charged a higher

CUPS & CONES

Small $4.75 $3.75
Medium $6.25 $5.25
Large $7.75 $6.75

Brownie $5.99 $4.47
Cookie $6.99 $5.47
Waffle $7.97 $6.47

price, customers would all choose the cheaper sundae and put the more expensive place out of business.

But we don't live in a perfectly rational world. In reality, saving money isn't the only reason we choose one thing over another. In chapter 4, we'll learn more about how we make financial choices, both good and bad.

THE ECOGNOMEICS OF THE SUPPLY CHAIN

When companies want to bring new products to market, things can get very complicated. The supply chain for a product includes all the designs, materials, parts, manufacturing, packaging, and shipping that a company has to plan for to turn ideas and raw materials into something that's ready for you to buy.

Ralph makes garden gnomes. You know, the little guys with the red hats? His company is called Something to Come Gnome To. For his gnomes, Ralph needs concrete and paint. He uses a Concrete Gnome Squirter to squirt wet concrete into a gnome-shaped mold and uses brushes to paint those charming faces.

Ralph's supply chain includes where the concrete mix is quarried; where his Concrete Gnome Squirter, gnome mold, and brushes are manufactured; and where his paints are developed.

For goods like cars and digital devices, the supply chain is international. The design might be created in one country, using metals and plastics from several other countries, all put together into the finished product in yet another country.

Consumers don't see how the supply chain works until something happens to interrupt it, like the COVID-19

pandemic that started in 2020.[30] Because many people were staying home, they stopped spending money on experiences like concerts, sporting events, and vacations and started buying stuff instead. Many of the things we buy are manufactured overseas or have parts that are manufactured overseas. They all come to the United States on enormous container ships that are unloaded at US ports and transported by trucks and trains across the country.

The international supply chain couldn't keep up with the overwhelming demand for stuff! There weren't enough raw materials, factories, ships, ports, or trucks to keep up, and workers were getting sick or being sent home due to pandemic rules about social distancing. Or, worse, they were being asked to work in dangerous conditions despite the risk to their health.

It isn't just global pandemics that put a stopper in the supply chain. In 2021, one of the world's largest container ships got stuck in the Suez Canal and shut down the shipping route for six days.[31] About 12 percent of global trade passes through the canal, which connects the Mediterranean Sea to the Red Sea, and the blockage held up over $9 billion in trade every day![32]

THAT'S SCARCELY APPROPRIATE

There's only so much stuff to go around, and everyone on Earth can't have it all. Even when it comes to that intangible stuff like video games, scarcity comes into play. There's no limit on the number of times your dragon-farming game can be downloaded because software can be reproduced over and over again with no extra materials needed. But you can't play without a device! The scarcity of materials to make laptops, gaming consoles, tablets, and phones affects the market for video games.

Sometimes, scarcity drives prices to ridiculous heights. Take the case of Beanie Babies, the little stuffed animals that come with a heart-shaped tag, created by the toy company Ty. In 1997, Beanie Babies sold for about $5. But somehow, people were willing to pay $300 or $400 for a small purple bear with a white rose embroidered on its chest.[33] Why?

Princess the purple bear was created after the death of Britain's Princess Diana, a royal figure beloved by many people around the world. To ensure that demand would be high for Princess, Ty only sent each store a dozen bears. Stores were left to decide how much to sell them for. In some cases, store owners held auctions and donated the money to local hospitals and animal shelters.

This scarcity was created by Ty, which often released new Beanie Babies and "retired" them after a while to boost the toys' value. For a while, Beanie Babies were considered investments: Buyers thought their value would only rise over time. Today, Princess wouldn't be your ticket to a life of wealth and ease. In 2022, Princess bears were selling online for between $10 and $40.[34]

Natural products can also become scarce because they can't be manufactured. Ambergris is a waxy substance produced in sperm whales' stomachs. It's like an incredibly expensive type of vomit. Ambergris washes up on shore around the world and has been used as a medicine, a spice, and an ingredient in perfume. Because it's rare and useful, it's highly valuable: In 2021, a lump of ambergris weighing 17 pounds was said to be worth over $1 million.[35] That price also reflects the fact that selling ambergris is illegal in some countries because sperm whales are a protected species.

AN INFLATED SENSE OF WORTH

Have you ever heard an older person talk about how much things used to cost? Usually it sounds like this: *Why, in my day you could get a cup of coffee for a quarter! A brand-new car cost $850!* Okay, they would've had to be alive and old enough to drive in 1908 to get a Model T Ford for $850,[36] but you get the picture.

Money loses its purchasing power over time. Coffee that cost 25 cents in 1970[37] costs a few dollars today, not because it's twelve or sixteen times better than it used to be but because of something called *inflation*. As money moves through the economy and more of it gets created through loans, people want to buy more—supply and demand again!

Inflation also happens over time as value gets added to raw materials, like when bits of metal and plastic get turned into your tablet or when ideas from an author's head get printed on paper and turned into a book. And when workers start to earn more money over time, it costs more to hire them, so prices rise.

None of this is necessarily bad, as long as inflation stays under control. The Federal Reserve, the central bank of the United States, has a couple of key jobs, and one of them is to manage inflation so that you won't have to listen to your grandkids complain about paying $8.5 million for a new car.

MARKET FAILURE PART 1: WHAT WE DON'T COUNT

Markets work pretty well for a lot of things, but they're not perfect. Sometimes the normal workings of the market lead to groups of people being worse off. This is known as *market failure*.³⁸ Companies have all kinds of costs to get products to market. Most ice cream parlors offer their customers things like plastic spoons and cups for to-go orders. Let's say you've tried to get rid of most of the single-use plastic at Brownie Sundays, but you do offer some reusable plastic cups and bowls that customers can take with them and then return later.

You buy these containers from a company called We're So Green that makes them from plastic pellets. The pellets come from a petrochemical company called Gunk. In the process of producing plastic pellets from oil, Gunk has been polluting a local river, causing illness in people and killing fish. Not so green!

None of the customers in this supply chain actually pay

for the cost of that devastation, not for the medical care for the people who got sick or unemployment for the people who used to make a living fishing or the "cost" of spoiling what used to be a healthy, functioning ecosystem.

This type of cost, which producers and consumers don't pay for, is called an *externality*. The cost is external; it's outside the price of making and selling brownie sundaes and plastic containers. The market doesn't figure in the cost of pollution. Total fail!

Some externalities aren't so terrible. A local fun fair might pay for a firework show for its customers, but plenty of people who didn't pay for a fun fair ticket will get to watch the show, too, because there's no way to control who can see the sky. That's spreading extra joy at no extra cost. Unless, of course, you can't stand fireworks. In that case, you might think about what you'd pay *not* to have to see or hear them.

MARKET FAILURE PART 2: WHO KNOWS MORE?

Another kind of market failure happens when one side in a business deal knows more than the other. In most transactions, each side knows what they're getting. This doesn't always happen.

Imagine that you want to buy your cousin's old bike. You take it for a test ride, and everything seems fine. You agree on a price and pay. The next day, when you want to take your bike for a ride, both tires are flat. What your cousin didn't tell you is that she pumped up the leaky tires just before you took that test ride. Now you've paid for a bike *and* you still need to get two new inner tubes. This is called *asymmetrical information*: Either the buyer or the seller has knowledge that lets them take advantage of the other.

MARKET FAILURE PART 3: TAKE A RIDE!

Do you know someone who's always willing to benefit from other people's generosity but doesn't pitch in themselves? Economists call these folks *free riders*. Free riders are happy to use services that they don't pay for and have a strong incentive to use more than their fair share.

Imagine that your teacher offers your class a movie day if the class average on a spelling test is above 80 percent. Your teacher hopes it will give everyone an incentive to study hard. Most of your classmates will cooperate, and some might even put in the time to help others who struggle with spelling.

However, one junior economist in the class is probably thinking, *I'll let everyone else put in the work because it doesn't matter if I get above 80 percent myself; it only matters that enough other kids get high scores.* That smarty-pants would get a free ride on movie day without having contributed any extra effort.

MIXED ECONOMIES AND MIXED FEELINGS

We said earlier that the United States has a mixed economy, with mostly private business and some institutions run by the government. But why should anyone care who runs a business? As long as things are getting done, what's the difference between an organization run by the government and one run by Joe's MegaBiz Inc.?

Believe it or not, people can get very excited and even very upset about public versus private business. Some people don't want the government to be involved in regulating private businesses or offering public services at all. Others wish the government in the United States played a bigger role in regulation and public services. This book isn't going to push you to think one way or the other, but I hope it will help you think critically about these issues.

One of the big differences between private and public businesses is that private businesses exist to create profits for their owners and investors. Investors can put their money directly into a company or through the stock market. That's a big topic, but basically, if a company wants to raise money, it can sell shares of its business to anyone who wants to invest. The shares are called *stock*. The stock market is the network where people buy and sell these shares. Investors can buy stock online or through a stockbroker, someone whose job it is to buy and sell shares for other people. Companies that sell shares on the stock market have a legal responsibility to create profits for their investors. If shareholders complain that a company isn't maximizing profits, the company can get in trouble.

Profit doesn't sound so bad—we all need money, after all! The problem comes when a company pursues profits at any cost, even the cost to things like the environment and human health, as we saw with Gunk, the plastics company. Or perhaps a private company might choose to skimp on safety measures and put its workers' lives in danger. Or only hire part-time employees to avoid paying extra benefits like health insurance and retirement.

Another problem with a completely private economy is that it leaves out people who have very low or no incomes. If every business needs to make profits, then every consumer has to spend money, and not everyone has the same amount of money to spend. We'll look more at inequality in chapter 6.

Government-run institutions, on the other hand, don't need to make money. They exist to provide services to people specifically in industries that aren't always profitable.

The problem here is that government services aren't always as quick to change or improve as private businesses. Public institutions usually need to do a lot more paperwork and have a lot more rules than private businesses. This is sometimes called *red tape*. The rules are there for good reasons, to make sure things are done accurately and fairly, but that often means that public industries are slower to solve problems than private companies.

You can see that there are good reasons to have a mix of private and public businesses. They're both good at different things. Having a thriving private sector in the economy means that you can take a risk and try your hand at making brownie sundaes for a living or invest in the next big tech company to hit the market. Having strong public services means that there are options when you need help or when private industry can't provide a solution.

SOMETHING FOR EVERYONE

What kinds of services might be run by government? Public schools, libraries, sewer systems, and bus services are usually run local governments. Other services are run by state governments, like your state parks and universities, or by the federal government, like NASA, the Centers for Disease Control and Prevention, and the national cheese stockpile we'll talk about in a moment. Government also runs the military. These are examples of public goods, things that are important to everyone but not always profitable.

If government-run businesses don't make profits, where do they get the money they need to operate? Easy: from you! Or, more accurately, from all of us. Anyone who works or has investments in the United States pays taxes. You pay income tax on the money you earn from work. You pay property tax if you own land or buildings, including houses. And you pay sales tax when you buy brownie sundaes. All this tax money goes to local, state, and federal governments to provide services (and collect cheese—I promise we'll get to that).

Governments also make rules that businesses have to follow. One example is the minimum wage, the lowest hourly wage a company can legally pay its employees. The US government, or federal government, sets one minimum wage; states and cities can set their own higher minimum wages—but they can't set lower minimum wages. Other regulations include health and safety laws, anti-discrimination laws, and licenses for certain types of businesses.

Governments can put money into some parts of the economy through subsidies. A subsidy is money the government pays directly to businesses to help keep prices low. A tax break, or paying lower taxes, is another type of subsidy. In 2020, the fossil fuel industry—coal, oil, and natural gas—received $5.9 trillion in subsidies from the US government,[39] making fossil fuels very profitable. You can decide for yourself if that's a real public good.

Governments can also subsidize industry by buying a lot of its product. This can help to increase supply by giving the industry a reason to invest in more equipment, land, workers, and so on. Famously, the US dairy industry makes more milk than Americans consume in a year. While milk has a short shelf life, cheese—especially processed cheese—can last much longer.

To help dairy farmers make money, the government buys cheese and stores it for the future: That's our national cheese stockpile. Before you wonder how the heck this is a public good, some of that cheese goes to food banks and other food programs. In 2018, the stockpile contained nearly 1.4 billion pounds of cheese.[40] If it were a single cheese wheel, it would be about as large as the US Capitol building! Pretty cheesy.

CHAPTER THREE

How Do We Earn and Spend Money?

BREAKFAST O'S
BREAKFAST O'S
BREAKFAST O'S
ALT MILK DRINK
ALT MILK DRINK
ALT MILK DRINK

So far, we've looked at what money is and how money systems work. Now let's take a closer look at how we make money and what we spend it on.

Making money isn't everything, but you'll need it to pay for food, clothes, housing, transportation, and just about everything else. That means eventually you'll need a job.

Picture your future self. We'll call you Future You. Present You, or the you who is reading this book right now, might not care too much about unemployment insurance and Medicare taxes, but Future You wants a nice life, and they're counting on Present You (or Just a Little Bit Older You) to make good choices!

So what are your options? You can work for yourself by starting your own business, or you can get a job and work for someone else. You might work for a company or an institution like a university or local, state, or federal government. We don't have room to explore all the different careers here, but let's look at a few things that you might want to think about when you're wondering what kind of work to choose.

A REAL BENEFIT

Most workers in the United States are employed by someone else. Working for a company or other organization means that the worker earns wages in return for working for a certain amount of time or doing certain tasks. For most jobs, full-time employment in the United States means working forty hours a week.

Why might you want to work for a company instead of for yourself? Sometimes it's just easier—running a business takes a lot of time and effort, and many businesses fail. There are other hidden reasons it can be nice to work for someone else: A full-time job in a company or government usually comes with benefits like health insurance, paid vacation and sick days, and a way to save for retirement.

If Future You gets sick and needs to stay at home, paid sick days mean that you won't lose money. Paid vacation means you can enjoy time traveling or just kicking around at home and still get paid! And because most health insurance in the United States is private, having a good health plan through your job is one of the best ways to make sure that when Future You needs to visit the doctor, you won't have to pay all the costs yourself.

WORK FOR YOURSELF (KIND OF)!

Some workers aren't really employees of the company they work for. In the age of app-based services like ride-hailing and grocery delivery, more and more people are becoming gig workers who are paid by the number of rides they give or deliveries they make. It's hard to track gig workers, but in 2021, 16 percent of all American adults had gotten work from a gig platform at some point.[41]

Gig workers don't have set hours, and they don't typically receive benefits like insurance or paid time off. They use their own cars and pay for their own gas and car insurance. This makes hiring gig workers very attractive to companies who want to save money. The upside for the workers is the flexibility: They can choose when to work and work as much or as little as they want.

Sometimes, though, it's not really a choice. Many gig workers do app-based work on top of working regular jobs. They have very little control over what they get paid. A real employee can usually ask for and negotiate raises, but gig workers can't. Some employees join unions, or groups that push for better conditions or more money. Gig workers in various cities and states have tried to unionize, but the companies they work for fight these efforts.[42]

Gamers and other content creators who make a living on platforms like Twitch or YouTube are freelance workers as well. Channels that draw in enough viewers can get paid by advertisers or by the platform company itself, but they have some of the same problems as gig workers, including a lack of benefits and no power over their pay.

WORK FOR YOURSELF (FOR REAL)!

In 2020, nearly 15 million workers in the United States were self-employed.[43] Self-employed people can work alone or own a company that hires other people. The difference between a self-employed person and a gig worker is that self-employed workers usually find work and negotiate fees on their own without being tied to the rate of pay set by an app.

Self-employment can be flexible, but it can also be demanding. You're in charge of everything, but that means . . . *you're in charge of everything.* Like gig workers, self-employed people in one-person businesses have to pay for their own health insurance and save for retirement, and they don't get any paid vacation or sick days. They have to be good at record-keeping and following through on tasks *and* be good at their actual jobs! Maybe it's time to take up dragon farming?

DISCRIMINATION

Having a secure, well-paying job with good benefits is a real accomplishment, but things aren't all rosy when it comes to work. Certain groups are discriminated against in various ways, from lower pay to employers' ideas about what hairstyles and expressions of gender identity are acceptable in the workplace.

Overall, women make less money than men, about 82 cents for every dollar earned by a man.[44] This gets worse when we break it down by race. Compared to white men, Black women earn 64 cents per dollar and Hispanic women earn 57 cents per dollar.[45]

The Americans with Disabilities Act requires employers to make "reasonable" changes in the workplace to help disabled employees do their jobs,[46] but employers don't always follow the rules. In 2021, a Walmart employee with Down syndrome was awarded over $125 million when she sued her employer for discrimination[47] because Walmart refused to accommodate her need for a predictable work schedule.

Transgender and nonbinary employees are often discriminated against when employers don't use their correct name or pronouns or when they're not allowed to use the right bathroom for their gender identity.⁴⁸ Black women have faced discrimination at work and been called "unprofessional" for wearing their hair naturally instead of conforming to white beauty standards. In 2020, the Supreme Court decided that discrimination against trans employees is illegal,⁴⁹ and California was the first state to make it illegal to discriminate against natural hairstyles.⁵⁰

We've seen how markets and employment work. But does the system work for everyone? We'll explore that question later on in chapter 6, but for now, we should remember that markets don't have morals. They're not good or bad in themselves, and they can't answer our questions about fairness or justice or who deserves a healthy, comfortable life and who doesn't. All a market can do is get goods and services to the people who are willing to pay for them.

THE HUMAN ECONOMY

So far, it sounds like economics is all about money. We keep using that word! In reality, not all trade involves money, and not all our relationships with other people are business relationships.

We have all kinds of interactions with people, and we give and accept gifts constantly to keep those relationships and make them stronger. You give a pencil to a classmate who needs one, but you don't demand an eraser in return (I hope). Later on, your classmate might share something with you at lunch or help you with a difficult science project.

These are examples of the human economy, the informal system that we use to trade goods and services without using money, direct barter, or any real system of accounting. Your classmate isn't doing the mental math to figure out if one pencil is worth half a bag of chips. You're both acting out of a social norm that says everyone's better off if we help one another when we can.

Are you part of a human economy? Think of some ways you give and get things in your daily life that don't involve exchanging money. Do you do favors for friends, family members, or neighbors? Do they do favors in return for you?

A good job and smart spending can get you far, but you can get a lot further when you work on building your human economy as well as filling your wallet!

CHAPTER FOUR

How Do We Make Choices?

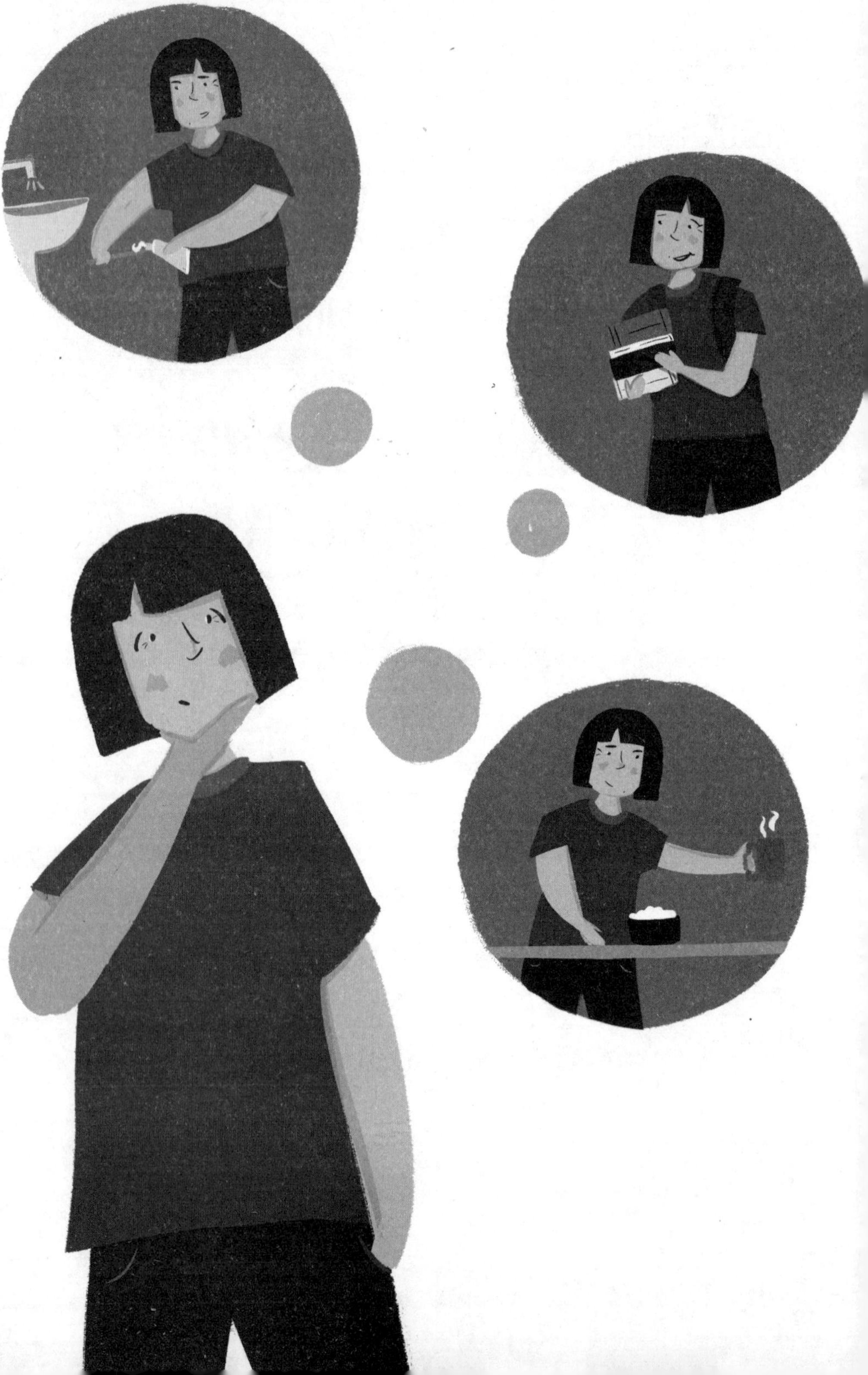

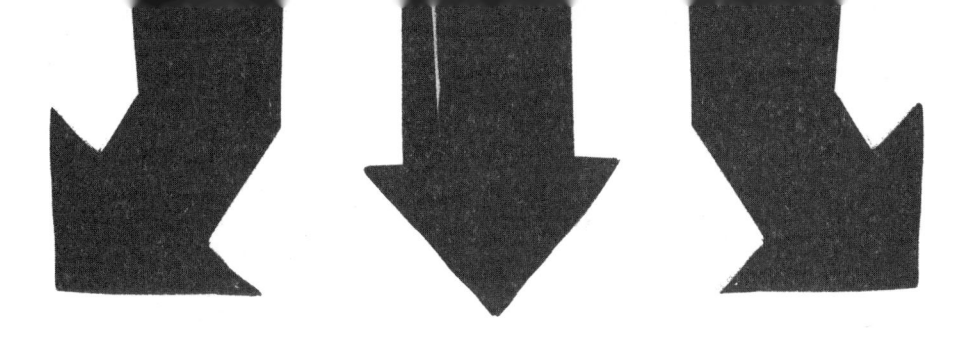

You make choices every day. You choose what to wear, what to eat for breakfast, if you're going to pay attention in class or goof off. You probably don't think of these as economic choices. But in a sense, they are! We use the same decision-making processes and concepts to make choices that involve money as we do for everything else.

A choice can make you better off, like when you choose to wear a warm coat on a cold day. Or it can make you worse off, like choosing to give your coat to a friend who forgot theirs at home. Are you thinking, *But what about the happiness I get from making someone else happy? Doesn't that make me better off?* Congratulations, you're already thinking like a behavioral economist![51]

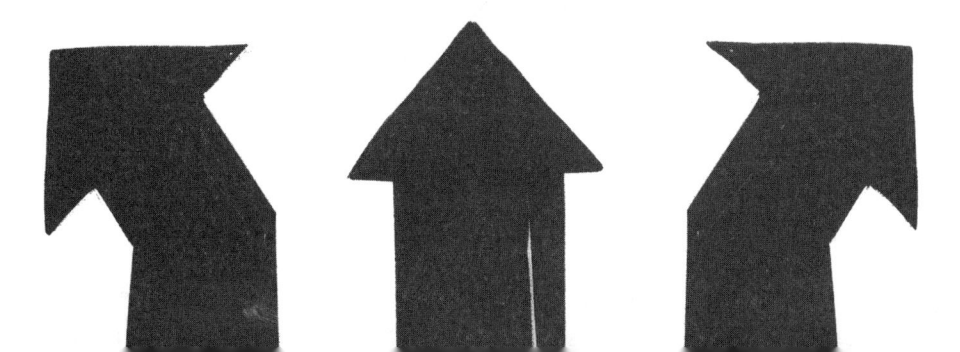

BEHAVE YOURSELF

Behavioral economics is a little different from everything we've been talking about up to this point. Regular, or standard, economics is all the supply-and-demand, price-and-market, buyer-and-seller stuff. Behavioral economics is like standard economics' smart-aleck sibling, the one who's always asking, *Oh yeah, how do you know?*

The focus of behavioral economics is in its name: It's looking at human behavior and trying to understand why we make the choices we make. In standard economics, we assume that people are making rational choices, which is to say, they think carefully about the economic choices they make. We also assume that people tend to prefer one thing over another and that they understand their preferences and make their choices based on what they prefer.

But that's not always true! In this chapter, we'll look at the many weird things that affect how we make choices.

UTILITY PANTS?

If you hang around economists for too long, eventually you'll hear them talking about how people *maximize their utility*. Huh?

We're not talking about utility knives or utility belts or things like that (although those might be useful for holding up your utility pants). When economists use the word *utility*, they mean "what you get out of something." If you want two things that each cost $5 but you can only afford one of them, you'll choose whichever one gives you the most utility, or whichever one you get the most out of.

Say you choose sparkly gel pens over a bottle of Magic Rust Fighter for your old bike chain. Standard economics looks at that choice like this: The utility you got from the pens (how useful or fun they are) was *worth more to you* than the utility you would have gotten from a clean bike chain. Doing your math homework in purple > riding your bike.

Behavioral economics looks at your choice and wonders about the other reasons you bought the pens. Maybe the store was having a sale and it looked too good to pass up. Maybe you knew you could use the pens right away, but you'd have to wait until the weekend to work on your bike. Or maybe there's always good music at the store that sells sparkly gel pens and it smells like strawberries, so it's a more enjoyable place to shop.

CHOOSE NOW!

We often choose to have something now rather than wait for something that might be better but will come around later. This is called present bias. Remember Present You and Future You from the last chapter? Present You is always trying to mess things up for Future You, even when Future You is just you tomorrow or next week!

Present You wants to spend, not save. Present You takes the thing that's being offered now, not the more interesting thing that's being offered later. Present You wants to jump up and down on the furniture instead of doing your homework because Present You isn't the one who has to worry about showing up to class without it. That's a problem for Future You!

It gets even harder when the potential rewards of waiting seem far away. Imagine that your teacher offers your class that movie day tomorrow or a week of movies in two months. Which one would you pick? What if your teacher offers you a movie day in four months or a movie week in six months? Is it easier to wait for the better offer if they're both so far in the future?

It isn't just kids who want things now. In the National Football League draft, teams can trade chances to pick a new player this year for a better position in the draft next year. For example, instead of a fourth-round pick this year, they might trade for a second-round pick next year, giving them the option to get a better player if they're willing to be patient. This makes sense if a manager is thinking long-term, but managers, like many of us, want to win now!

Most of the time, managers will take the best offer they can get today and leave next year's draft for Future Them to deal with!

WHAT AN OPPORTUNITY (COST)!

Have you ever wondered about parallel universes? You know, the idea that somewhere there are Parallel Yous walking around who made the choices Past You didn't make? In one parallel universe, you tried out for the pickleball team instead of taking clarinet lessons. In another universe, you dyed your hair pink instead of letting your grandpa give you a bowl cut. Economists might not spend much time talking about parallel universes, but they do talk about *opportunity cost*, which isn't too far off.

When you buy gel pens instead of Magic Rust Fighter, the opportunity cost of that choice is all the bike rides you didn't take because your chain was too rusted. If you choose movie day now instead of movie week later, the opportunity cost is four days of movies!

Thinking about opportunity cost can help you make more satisfying choices: What are you giving up when you choose A over B? Just remember, there's no avoiding opportunity costs. We can imagine universes where Parallel Yous have made every possible choice, but neither economists nor physicists have figured out how to get there yet.

SEEING THE SAME THING EVERYWHERE

If you're trying to choose which bike helmet to buy, you could spend a few days researching all the brands of helmets, comparing their safety information, their cost, and how comfortable they are. Or you might remember that your brother bought a helmet from a company called Bonkers last month and it seems just fine. And now that you think about it, you've seen a few other kids with the same helmet, so it's probably a good one. You buy it.

This is the *availability rule*. That's when we make

choices based on the information that's most available to us. When we buy things using the availability rule, we might choose something because people we know have bought it. We might also buy something that we've seen over and over in ads. When you were looking for a helmet, you went with one that was familiar to you. It was easy to recall the brand name. You didn't compare it to every other helmet; you made a guess that it was good because others are using it. The bike store near your house carries Bonkers helmets, which reinforces your idea that they must be good.

Here's another example of the availability rule: Your school recently lectured the students for an hour about the dangers of wearing wheelie shoes to school. You heard how many students were injured while rolling down hallways and saw a picture of someone with a broken arm after an accident involving wheelie shoes. The next day, you put on your new helmet and ride to school, feeling good about your choice to ride a bike and not wear wheelie shoes.

In reality, far more kids are seriously injured in bike accidents every year than in wheelie shoe accidents, and not just because bikes are more common. The percentage of accidents for bikes is higher, too. However, because you've learned about wheelie shoe accidents but not bike accidents, you think the shoes are more dangerous.

Keep this in mind when you're making choices: We can't research every single decision endlessly, but ask yourself if you're only making a choice based on what you already know.

LOOKS GOOD TO ME

Your brother's bike helmet is black with a thin neon-green streak along each side. It looks sporty, and when he's wearing it, he looks like a pro cyclist. You would also like to look like a pro, so you buy the same helmet because it matches your idea of what a good helmet should look like: sporty and cool. This is your brain using the *representativeness rule*:

The black-and-green helmet *looks* like what you think a helmet should look like, even though you know nothing about how safe or comfortable it is.

THE PRICE IS RIGHT

You know that your brother paid $20 for his helmet, so you expect to pay the same. But what would you pay for a helmet if you had no idea what your brother had paid for his? If you didn't have that information, you might pay $40 for the same helmet. After all, you're already convinced that it's the best one. But because you know he paid $20, you'd feel ripped off if a store charged $40 for the same helmet. That's called *anchoring*: The price you're willing to pay is anchored, or tied, to the price you expected.

Anchoring has another interesting effect. Ask someone what year World War I started (the answer is 1914). Separately, so they can't hear the first person's answer, ask a second person what year World War II started (it's 1939). Then ask each of them what they'd be willing to pay for your latest and greatest piece of school artwork.

Even though answering a question about a historical date has nothing to do with what you'd pay for a drawing, the person who answered the question about WWII should give a slightly higher figure than the person who answered the question about WWI *because they were already thinking of a higher number.* (Note: It helps to ask two people who are similar in their knowledge and spending power. Your mom and your little sister have very different ideas about the value of money.)

IT HURTS TO LOSE

Everyone at school is playing a new fruit-themed trading-card game called Friendly Fruit. Your friend wants to build their card collection, and they're willing to pay cash. You have a durian card, the pride of your collection. (Durian is a famously smelly but delicious fruit native to Southeast Asia.)

The official Friendly Fruit price guide says it's worth $10. But you love this card. You've spent many hours displaying it in your room, taking selfies with it, and gazing at its loveliness. You won't sell it for anything less than $25. Your desperate friend pays up, and you're $25 richer. But you miss your durian card. You want another. Luckily, your cousin is offering a durian card for $25. Do you buy it?

A traditional economist might say yes. If you thought the card was worth $25 when you sold it, you should also be willing to pay $25 for it. But officially it's only worth $10! You know that you'd be paying $15 more than the card is worth. You decide you can live without another durian card.

What's going on here? The fancy term is *loss aversion*. It means that we feel the pain of a loss (the loss of the card you spent so many happy hours with) more than we feel the joy of gaining the same thing (an identical durian card). Gaining a new card would have felt good, but losing *your* card made you feel "double bad." That's why you charged more to sell your card than you were willing to pay to buy it yourself.

This feeling is especially strong because we tend to care more about things we already own.

That's called the *endowment effect*. Your durian card was worth more to you than your cousin's identical durian card *because it was yours*. Same goes for your dog, who is, to you, better than any other dog anywhere.

WHAT DID YOU EXPECT?

If you bought gel pens at the strawberry-scented mall store, you enjoyed the shopping experience for reasons that have nothing to do with how well the pens work or their price. But sometimes it works the other way. Feeling like we got a good deal—or not—affects how we think about what we bought.

You love yard sales! So much cheap stuff! Just last week, you bought the third book in the Franken-wombat series at a yard sale for 50 cents. A new copy costs $15.99 plus tax. Fifty cents was a steal. You enjoyed reading it so much, you're planning to buy the fourth book at a bookstore later today, and you're willing to pay the full price. Now you see a like-new copy of Franken-wombat 4 at another yard sale. The kid at the cash table tells you it costs $15.99 plus tax.

You try to bargain. You wouldn't bargain at a bookstore, but everyone expects bargaining at a yard sale. The kid refuses. What do you do?

You wouldn't lose anything if you bought the book from the yard sale because you were already planning to spend exactly that amount on the same book at a store.

But if you buy something at full price from a yard sale, you lose the giddy feeling that you got a great deal. You didn't pay more than you were *willing* to pay, but you did pay more than you *expected* to pay.

This is why some stores run "sales" all the time: Shoppers like to think they're getting a good deal, and sometimes that influences their choice to buy something even more than the actual price of the thing they're buying. Pay attention the next time you're in a store. What's on sale? How often is that item on sale, and what's the regular price? Do you or your family members buy things just because they're on sale?

Sometimes we spend *more* money on something because we're in a certain setting. The same soda costs more at a fancy resort than at a vending machine, but at the resort, you're also paying for atmosphere. You expect to pay more, so it doesn't bother you as much. But remember, Future You might be watching and wishing you'd waited to buy a cheaper soda from the shabby store around the corner from the resort.

JUST STOP IT!

What about choosing to stop doing something? That's a tricky choice, too!

Say you start accordion lessons. You've been wanting to learn how play a polka for a long time. But you don't enjoy the accordion as much as you thought you would. And your elbow is starting to hurt from all that squeezing.

Should you stop your lessons and spend those precious hours doing something else? Or should you keep going just because you've already put so much time into it? This is the idea of *sunk costs*.

You've already sunk money and time into your lessons, and you'll never get them back. The way to think about it isn't to look to the past but to look ahead. Will you (and your sore elbow) ultimately be glad if you quit now, or will you regret it?

Sunk costs bother us more early on, when we first feel like we're wasting our money if we don't use something we've already paid for. If you decide to give up on your accordion lessons, you might feel very bad about it for the first week and then a little bad for a month, and after that, you might not think about it at all. Quitting your lessons is probably the right choice in this case.

Here's something to think about: If you were an economics teacher, would you give credit to a student who used sunk costs to argue that they should quit doing homework?

NUDGE, NUDGE

Economics has a nickname: the dismal science. It can be pretty dismal to think about inequality and ruining the environment in the name of profit, which we'll look at in the next couple of chapters. But for this section, let's think of economics as the sneaky science.

We've seen some examples of how economic principles affect our choices. So how can we make better choices? And is it all up to us, or should someone figure out how to make it easier to choose wisely? This is the idea behind *nudging*. Nudges make good choices easy.

If you've ever stepped in dog poop on the sidewalk or rolled over it in your wheelchair, you might have wondered why some dog walkers don't seem to care about what their pups' behinds leave behind. Are they just careless, or did they forget to bring a plastic bag? Were they heading to meet a friend for coffee and didn't want to show up holding a bag of dog poop? Having access to trash cans and free bags for picking up and disposing of poop is an easy nudge for cleaner streets.

New Taipei City in Taiwan went even further: Residents who disposed of dog poop in special containers were automatically entered in a lottery to win up to $2,000. Suddenly, sidewalk poop was cut in half! Okay, not literally—the amount of poop on sidewalks was cut down by 50 percent.

You probably come across nudges all the time without realizing it. Putting fruit where it's easy to grab in the lunch line is a nudge: *This is good for you! Go ahead and take one!* So is having a food-waste bin in your kitchen: *Don't throw food scraps into the regular trash! Make compost!* A food-sharing table in the cafeteria is a great nudge: *Don't ditch the pudding that came with your lunch! Leave it here for someone who does want it!*

Nudges can work for bad choices, too. Why would anyone want to make it easier for people to make the wrong choice? You guessed it: when they can get money out of it! All those in-app purchases for your favorite games aren't there by accident. Game companies know that you're more likely to click to buy a special tool if you're in the middle of playing because you can see immediately how useful it will be. They also know that you're more likely to make in-app purchases if you already have a credit card or online payment method attached to your account: the magic of the single click.

What's sneakier than a nudge? *Sludge.* Where nudges make choices easy, sludge makes them hard. Have you heard a family member complain about how hard it is to return something they bought online or to stop a subscription they no longer want? When a company makes it hard to get your money back by sending you to multiple different websites or requiring you to call their customer service department and spend an hour on hold, that's sludge.

Sludge isn't just for businesses, either. Some states have passed laws that require voters to show certain types of identification at the poll. Other laws limit mail-in voting. In some areas, polling places have closed, making the lines at other poll sites longer. This makes voting harder.

When we vote, we're choosing the government and the laws that affect our lives, so when voting gets harder, not everyone gets a say. One study showed that after many of these laws were passed, over 70 percent of eligible white voters cast ballots compared to less than 60 percent of Black voters.[52] That's not just a sneaky science; that's a kind of sludge that plugs up our democracy.

CHAPTER FIVE

What Do We Value?

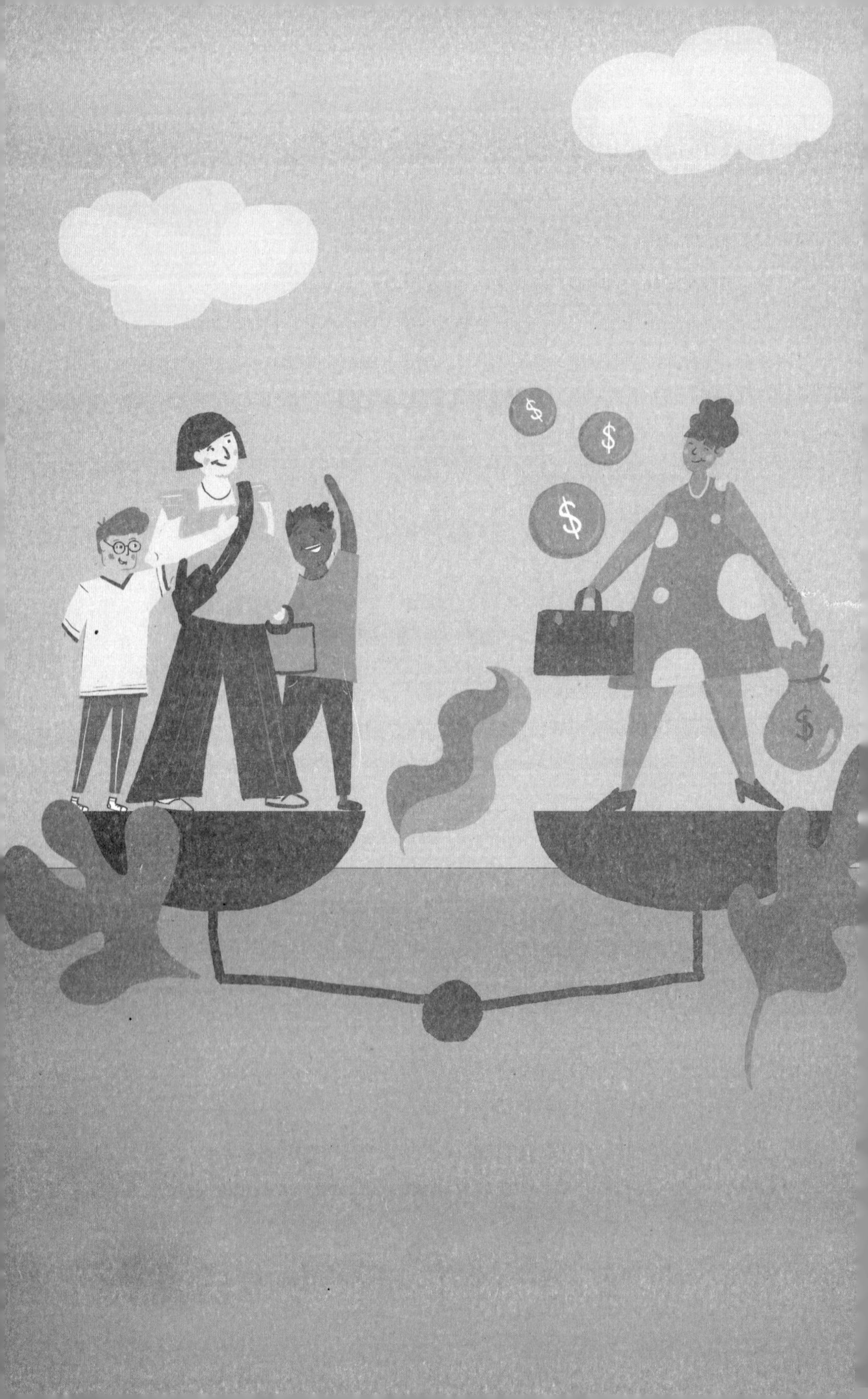

alue is a word we use in a lot of different ways. It's not always about money.

We say that a large box of cereal is a better value than a small box. That's definitely about money. Your teachers probably tell you about the value of a college education. That might be about money because college graduates earn more over their lives than those who don't go to college, but it's also about the knowledge and experiences college can bring. When we talk about "our values," we're usually talking about things that can be completely separate from money, like honesty, integrity, and kindness.

If you've been paying attention so far, you know that even when something doesn't seem to be about economics, economists will tell you that it is! Just as economics affects all kinds of choices in our lives, it gives us new ways to look at value: not just the value we can get for our money, but all our values.

THE VALUE OF EVERYTHING

Tune into the news for long enough, and someone will mention three letters: *GDP*. They stand for *gross domestic product*, and no, you're not the only one to start thinking of poop jokes when you hear that phrase. In this case, though, *gross* means "total." GDP measures the total size of an economy.

A country's GDP is the sum of all the goods and services it produces.[53] It's everything you buy, everything your family buys, everything every business in your town buys, and so on. You can see how, with this measurement, the economy grows when businesses and people spend more money.

Keep listening to the news, and you might hear something like "GDP was up 2 percentage points in the last quarter." (I'm just making that up.) What it means is that the economy has grown by 2 percent in the past three months.

When the economy grows, we typically think it's a good thing because when people and businesses spend more money, other people and other businesses get more money! A growing economy usually means more jobs, and that leads to more people with money to spend and more growth and, well, you can see the pattern.

When growth slows down, economists get pretty doom-and-gloomy because usually that means fewer jobs and less money to go around.

We're wading into some pretty deep economic waters here. GDP? Growth? How is this stuff interesting? Does the author of this book really think another poop joke is going to make up for a chapter of boredom?

You could go your whole life without thinking about economic growth, and you'd be just fine. Even Future You doesn't have to spend any time studying GDP graphs if they don't want to. But here's why we're looking at it: It's not about the things it counts, it's about everything it *doesn't* count.

In this chapter, we're looking for clues to all the things that matter in our lives and seeing how they show up in the economy. And *that's* important because when it comes to making change, governments and organizations like to look where the money is.

THE VALUE OF EVERYTHING
(BUT ONLY THINGS THAT COST MONEY)

GDP is a useful measurement, but it's sort of like your GPA. It tells someone exactly one thing. Your GPA says how well (or how poorly) you do on tests, homework, and classwork, but it doesn't say that you didn't turn in your homework because you were so busy helping a friend that you didn't have time to finish. It doesn't say that you work your hardest when you're faced with a challenge or that you always try to make others feel included. Your GPA doesn't measure your worth as a person!

Similarly, GDP measures the size of an economy, but it has nothing to say about where that money is going or what it does. It doesn't measure our quality of life. If one company spends $10 million on developing an important new vaccine and another company spends $10 million on spreading misinformation about vaccines to scare people and keep them from getting vaccinated, GDP still grows by $10 million in each case!

Another unfortunate example comes from cleaning up after disasters. Having pristine, healthy ecosystems doesn't add to a country's GDP. But if an oil pipeline leaks and pollutes the local environment, the cost of cleaning it up counts as economic growth. Now, that's a disaster.

An economy can actually grow when a small number of people hold most of the wealth and large numbers of people live in poverty. Remember, markets aren't naturally fair.

GDP doesn't even measure all the work we do! It only measures work that someone does for pay. If your little sister goes to a childcare center during the day, the fees add to economic growth. If your dad stays home and cares for her, GDP doesn't budge, even though he's putting in the same work as a childcare provider. Try using this argument to convince your parents they should hire your brother to clean your room: It's better for the economy!

WONDERING ABOUT NATURAL WONDERS

Let's take a closer look at this contrast between economic value and other values.

In order to make a profit, companies need to know what they're spending. Ralph, our gnome artist from chapter 2, keeps detailed records of how much he spends on concrete. To make things simple, let's say that Ralph buys his dry concrete mix directly from the manufacturer, Clumpy Concrete.

Clumpy Concrete keeps track of its costs, too: the sand, gravel, and other materials that go into the mix; the equipment it needs to quarry its raw materials; the factory and machinery that transform the raw materials into its special garden gnome concrete mixture; and the water and energy it uses to run its equipment.

Everyone's tracking money, but are they really tracking the full cost of concrete? We know from chapter 2 that companies don't include externalities like CO_2 emissions or water pollution in their financial records. (Eight percent of all human carbon emissions come from the concrete industry![54]) But what about at the beginning of the process: Does Clumpy Concrete include the true value of the raw materials it uses to manufacture concrete mix in its list of costs?

Limestone is one of the components of concrete.[55] In parts of the Earth that were underwater hundreds of millions of years ago, limestone formed as the calcium-rich shells of ancient sea creatures fell to the seafloor and were compressed into stone over time.[56] Nature spent longer making limestone than humans have spent making concrete, but you won't find any mention of the cost of nature's time, energy, or materials. In economic terms, the services provided by Earth are free, and our only costs are buying land and equipment and hiring labor.

In a way, this makes sense. Should you have to pay for the cost of having a solid surface to walk on every time your feet touch bare earth? Do you pay for air every time you take a breath? Dirt and air took a long time to make, too! But that would get expensive quickly. How would we keep track of it, anyway? Who would we pay, and how would we pay it?

But we run into problems when we treat the planet like an all-you-can-eat buffet. Sand is another of the natural resources we use to make concrete. So much sand has been dredged from the bottom of Poyang Lake in China that now too much water flows out to the Yangtze River and the lake's water level is falling. This makes life harder for the migratory birds that visit each year, the porpoises who can't see through all the sediment stirred up by mining, and the people who used to make a living fishing from the lake.[57]

Once we've used a natural resource like limestone, water, or sand, we can't just order more from the factory. Our scale of manufacturing things is so much faster than Earth's scale, there's no way Earth can catch up to human activity. As we make more concrete for more bridges, dams, buildings, and garden gnomes, our economy grows. In theory, our economy could grow forever—but nature's factory can't.

It's not just environmental "goods" like sand and limestone that industries rely on. Ecosystem services are important natural processes, like the way forests and grasslands keep carbon out of the atmosphere and how wetlands filter our water. Our planet provides us with all the basics we need—air, water, soil, a habitable climate—free of charge, and all we have to do is make sure we don't mess it up.

VALUABLE OR PRICELESS?

Why would we want to put a price on "priceless" things? What good would it do to say that ecosystem services are worth $33 trillion, as an environmental economist did back in 1997?[58] Economists argue about that number (they love to argue), but the idea is that we pay more attention to things we can put a price on.

We know the dollar value of the fishing industry along our coasts, so we can figure out the value of the ecosystem services the coastal environment provides. The "cost" of the coast's services isn't part of the cost your family pays when you buy fish, but if we understand how much the coast is valued in dollars, we might treat it like the precious resource it is.

Some governments have started making direct payments to landowners to preserve forests and other valuable ecosystems instead of letting them be clear-cut or built up. Costa Rica has paid more than 18,000 landowning families in its ecosystem services program.[59]

It's worth asking about the unintended side effects of programs that pay landowners not to cut down forests: Does money change how they would have behaved otherwise? If one landowner is in a payment program and another isn't, is the landowner who isn't getting paid more likely to cut down trees? One study showed that many people who participated in the program were getting payments for land they weren't planning to clear anyway.[60]

THE POWER OF SLOWING DOWN

Another way to handle environmental costs is to make consumers pay more. This can be done by increasing prices or by adding a tax. Taxes are a tool the government uses to bring in money, but they can also be used to encourage certain kinds of activities and discourage others. For example, if your parents drive a gasoline-powered car, they're paying a gas tax every time they fill up. If they bought an electric car, they might have gotten a tax credit, *and* they no longer have to pay the gas tax. The idea behind both of these things is good old supply and demand: In theory, if prices rise, demand should drop.

That's great when we want to stop using one resource, like oil, and use something else instead, like electricity generated from renewable sources. When we say a resource is renewable, we mean that we can grow or create more of it within a useful human time frame: We can grow more trees for lumber, and we can make wind power as long as the wind blows and solar power as long as the sun shines.

We can't make more oil, natural gas, or limestone within a human lifetime or even a few human lifetimes. (If you're wondering how we can grow more limestone, the answer is, we're doing it right now; it just won't be gnome-ready for a few hundred million years.) By putting a tax on oil and natural gas and even paying people subsidies to use solar power, we might be able to slow down or stop using the carbon-based fuels that are causing climate change.

We might be able to "green" the concrete industry by using renewable energy in manufacturing and recycling some concrete to make new building materials.[61] But at the moment we don't have a renewable substitute for concrete or all the sand and stone we need to make it. We can't make our modern bridges and skyscrapers out of wood or bamboo, unfortunately.

But economics is all about *the efficient allocation of resources*. What's more efficient: saving our precious non-renewable resources for the things we really need them for or using them to make garden gnomes? Sorry, Ralph.

THE TRUE COST

A small nonprofit organization in the Netherlands, True Price, is finding ways include all those externalities in the prices of goods.[62] The group worked with a Dutch grocery store to calculate the true costs of various items and display both side by side. A shopper can easily see what they're *not* paying for at a typical grocery store when they buy tomatoes, milk, or meat. The true price reflects environmental and social costs like carbon emissions, water use, and how workers are treated and paid.

Shoppers can then decide if they want to pay the lower price or the higher, true price. If they choose to pay the true price, the extra money goes to fund projects that help to fix environmental and social problems. One estimate found that the true cost of the food system in the United States is nearly three times as large as the costs we actually pay![63]

It's clever to show consumers what things really cost, but the producers are the ones who can make changes to the whole system. Knowing the true prices of goods could help companies lower those "external" costs, making things better for the environment and their workers at the same time.

TWO KINDS OF GREEN

Green business is big business. Manufacturers and advertisers know that consumers care about the environment and are willing to pay more for sustainable products. You can buy 100 percent recycled toilet paper and "sustainable" water bottles made from recycled plastic.[64] Even oil companies are eager to let us know that they're working toward our "low-carbon" future![65]

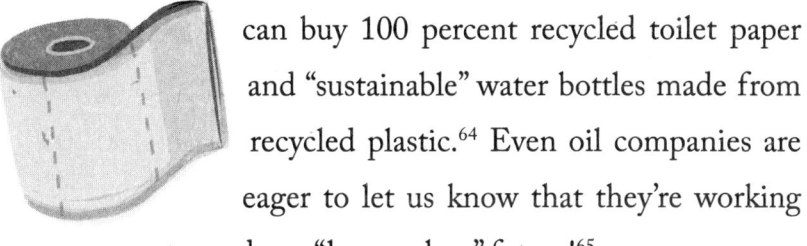

Unfortunately, a study of European companies showed that 42 percent of green statements like these were exaggerated or false.[66] When corporations mislead their customers by pretending to be more environmentally friendly than they really are, it's called *greenwashing*. Why would a company lie about something as important as preserving our natural world? The answer is all about that other kind of green: money.

IS IT WORTH IT?

Is there a limit to how much the world's economy can grow? Does it have to keep growing?

This is another one of those issues that people have very strong feelings about. It's often framed as two opposing ideas: the economy versus the environment. Jobs versus spotted owls.[67] When old-growth forests in the Pacific Northwest were closed to logging in order to protect the endangered northern spotted owl, timber companies claimed 130,000 jobs could be lost. Environmental activists were criticized for caring more about animals than humans.

It seems like an argument with no solution, but things that are set up as either-or situations are usually too simplistic to show the truth. Here are some questions that are worth thinking about:

> 1. WE CAN'T HAVE AN ECONOMY WITHOUT AN ENVIRONMENT, SO HOW CAN WE WORK WITHIN OUR "PLANETARY BOUNDARIES" TO LIVE GOOD LIVES *AND* TAKE CARE OF OUR ONLY HOME?

> 2. ARE WE RESPONSIBLE FOR LEAVING FUTURE GENERATIONS WITH THE SAME ABUNDANT RESOURCES WE HAVE TODAY SO THAT THEY CAN HAVE A DECENT QUALITY OF LIFE, TOO?

Thinking this way doesn't mean there won't be problems. People did lose logging jobs over the spotted owl, but the losses were less than a quarter of what the timber industry had feared. As we'll see in the next chapter, economics can give us tools to take care of people as the world of work changes.

EVERYTHING WE VALUE

One more thought about GDP: We said it isn't supposed to measure our quality of life, but, as people say in the business world, "What gets measured gets managed."[68] Should we try to find other ways to measure the well-being of the planet and everyone on it?

One small country is famous for trying this. Bhutan, a Himalayan nation of less than 800,000 people,[69] measures its gross national happiness. GNH takes thirty-three measurements, including education level, health, and how people use their time, and uses the results to set government policies.[70]

Interestingly, Bhutan was also the first country in the world to be carbon-negative, meaning that through a combination of renewable electricity and maintaining its forests, it's able to sequester more carbon than it produces.[71]

You can take stock of your own values and measure your

well-being by asking yourself what your real needs are and what your wants are. Everyone on Earth should be able to have what they need, and we should all have a shot at getting some of the things we want as well. But those "things" don't always have to be consumer goods. They don't always have to use up scarce resources or create waste. Some of the things we enjoy most are experiences, and many experiences are free.

We don't have to rely on one number to tell us how well our lives are going or the state of the planet. In fact, any single number will fail to show us all the complexity of our world and puts us at risk of misunderstanding what we should value most.

CHAPTER SIX

Why Doesn't Everyone Have Enough?

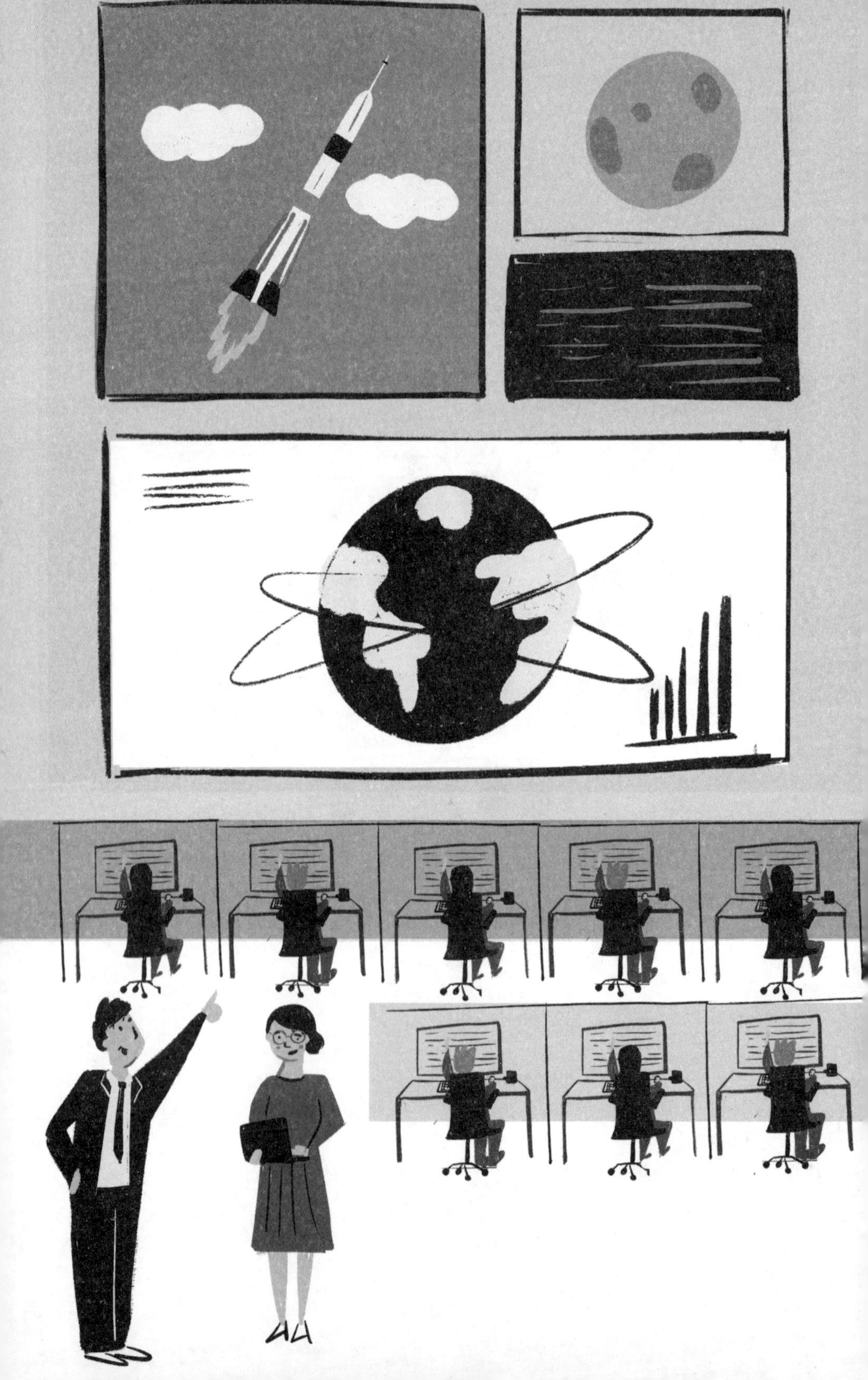

On July 11, 2021, a history-making rocket flight launched from the New Mexico desert. Richard Branson, the billionaire owner of Virgin Galactic, became the first person to fly into space in a craft built by his own private space travel company.[72] Nine days later, another billionaire launched into space.[73] Jeff Bezos, the founder of Amazon, was the wealthiest person in the world at the time of his flight. Afterward, Bezos thanked his Amazon employees and customers, saying, "You guys paid for all this."[74]

Bezos was worth more than $200 billion[75] around the time of his flight. The average salary of an Amazon warehouse or transportation employee was around $17 an hour.[76] At that rate, a warehouse employee would have to work over 11 billion hours to equal the wealth of Jeff Bezos.

The theme of this chapter isn't "billionaires in space," but these stories illustrate an important question: Why do some people have enough money to build their own rockets while others struggle to pay for basic things like food and shelter?

The larger question is: What is economic inequality? Does it matter, and if so, what should we do about it?

SANDWICH INEQUALITY

What's the first thing you think when you hear the word *inequality*? The rich and the poor? The haves and the have-nots? You're on the right track, but it's not just about the difference between someone who owns a superyacht and someone who can't afford a car. Economic inequality is about the unequal distribution of wealth across all of society and why a small group of people at the top has much, much more money than everyone else.

Have you heard the saying *The rich get richer and the poor get poorer*? There's a lot of truth to that in America. The United States has greater inequality than other wealthy industrialized countries,[77] and the gap is growing.

In the twentieth century, economic mobility, or the possibility of earning more money than your parents, was central to the American Dream. Over 90 percent of children born in the 1940s earned more money as adults than their parents had. Today, only about 50 percent of kids make that goal.[78]

Why? Because even though the American economy is growing, that growth isn't being shared equally. The pie is getting bigger, but a smaller number of people are taking more of it, leaving less for the rest.

In 1917, the richest 1 percent of Americans had about 18 percent of the national income, or the money that people make at their jobs and through their investments.[79] If that's hard to picture, imagine 100 kids and 100 sandwiches. The sandwiches represent income. The first kid in line takes 18 sandwiches, leaving 82 for the other 99 kids.

Income inequality peaked just before the stock market crash that began the Great Depression. In 1928, that first kid got to walk off with 24 sandwiches! During the Great Depression and for about fifty years after it, income inequality got lower and lower, down to about 9 percent in 1975. Where are we now? Inequality is rising again. As of 2015, we're letting that first kid get away with 22 sandwiches!

And that's just income. Wealth, or the money, property, and other valuable assets that people hold, is another way to measure inequality. Picture those 100 sandwiches: If they represent wealth, the first 10 kids in line get to take 70 sandwiches! The other 90 kids only have 30 sandwiches to share between them.[80]

MONEY, MONEY, MONEY

So why do the rich get richer? Starting life with money makes it easier to do the things that help you get more money: get a good education, get financial help from your family, borrow money to buy a house or expand a business, and meet the sort of people who also earn a lot of money.

But as we saw with the sandwiches, inequality isn't just about how much money someone earns for doing a job. Wealth matters here: People who have assets can use them to make more money.

One way to do this is through the stock market, the system that lets people invest money in companies that offer shares, or a percentage of ownership in the company. The goal of investing is to put your money into companies that are going to become more valuable. When you sell your shares, you make a profit.

If a share of a company costs $10 in 2000 and reaches a price of $20 per share in 2024, someone who invested $1 million in the company in 2000 will make more profit by selling their shares in 2024 than someone who only invested $100: That's just math. The same goes for someone who can afford to buy an expensive property versus someone who bought cheap property: The expensive property will probably go up more in value over time.

Coming from a wealthy family means that this wealth-building process has happened over generations, not just one person's lifetime. Families that can afford to pass down large inheritances to the next generation are setting their children up for success in a way that families without wealth can't do. Up to half the wealth in the United States was inherited, and most of that was inherited by the folks in the top 10 percent.[81]

Believe it or not, even animals can inherit wealth and its privileges from their parents! Red squirrel parents pass their lifetime savings of acorns and pine cones down to their children.[82] Animals can also pass on homes and tools to their kids. Clown fish inherit the right to hide in sea anemones, which gives the ones with the best hiding spots an advantage. Capuchin monkeys and chimpanzees have passed along their best tools to their young, sort of like getting your mom's old car for your sixteenth birthday. If you start life at the top, it's much easier to stay there, even if you're a fish.

Many tax laws favor wealth, too. If you invest in the stock market, you'll pay tax on any profits you make, but the percentage you'll pay on that profit is lower than the percentage you'll pay on income from a job. What this means is that a billionaire investor who makes his money through buying and selling stocks pays a lower tax rate than his executive assistant![83]

114 | BIG MONEY

Shouldn't people who run companies and create jobs be rewarded for making others better off? Higher wages for the higher-ups can encourage other workers to be more productive or efficient in order to get a promotion: good for the company, good for the employee. But should the CEO of a company earn 351 times as much as his employees?[84] That's the average difference between CEO pay and worker pay in the largest American companies.

(Why "his employees"? Only 41 of the chief executive officers of the 500 largest companies in the United States in 2021 were women,[85] and it's hard to find numbers on nonbinary and transgender CEOs.)

Working in finance can pay extremely well. The financial side of the economy includes banks and the stock market, commonly known as Wall Street, after the street where the New York Stock Exchange lives. Trading money for a living can make a fortune for the trader and their wealthy clients, but it doesn't often create opportunities for anyone else in the way that jobs in the "real" economy can.

Someone who invents a long-lasting and inexpensive battery for electric cars might also become fabulously wealthy, but their invention would bring some actual good to the rest of society, too. More people would be able to afford electric cars, and we'd cut down on fossil fuel use. Say this genius inventor also starts a company that sells affordable electric cars. Now they're providing jobs for people, which supports businesses where the workers live. The company and its workers would pay taxes, which would then support more services for everyone.[86]

The promise of extreme wealth in high finance lures clever and ambitious people away from jobs that have greater social benefits, but there's another problem, too. The reality of working with money is that it's literally your job to make that money grow, and that means putting profit first. There's even a special term for a type of investor who buys companies and then fires workers, sells property, and tries to squeeze all the value out of their investment no matter who it hurts: *vulture capitalist*.[87]

The point of this isn't to say that anyone who works in finance is bad, only that the choices we make about where to work have opportunity costs, too.

LAND OF OPPORTUNITY?

The story we tell ourselves in the United States is that wealth is a matter of personal responsibility. Anyone can get rich if they work hard enough! Right?

It might be possible for any one person to live the rags-to-riches story, coming from a humble background and rising to the dizzying heights of wealth. It's also possible for someone to make poor choices and struggle with money. But, again, that's not what we mean when we talk about inequality. It's not about personal choices or individual responsibility.

It's also not about stereotypes, like whether the rich are hardworking (or greedy) or the poor are lazy (or noble). When we think in stereotypes, we put the responsibility on individuals and ignore all the ways in which our society makes it hard for some people to get by and easy for others.

Most Americans, almost 90 percent, believe they're in the middle class,[88] even though that would be mathematically impossible! In America, the middle class is supposed to be the group that works hard, goes to college, owns a home, and retires comfortably. The problem is, that life is getting harder to achieve.

Why can't people who don't have enough money just get better jobs, spend smarter, and get ahead? Sometimes they can! But saving and spending smarter are tough when prices for those middle-class necessities rise. College education[89] and health care[90] are getting more expensive. So are buying a home[91] and sending kids to childcare.[92]

But most workers aren't seeing their wages rise in the same way.[93] Some employers did offer higher pay to attract workers during the COVID-19 pandemic, but many of those jobs were low-paid service jobs, and workers often still felt as if they were struggling to make ends meet.[94] And when the cost of living rose (due to inflation from problems in the supply chain), the squeeze on workers got even worse.

This leaves families with less money to save for retirement, to pass on to the next generation, or to cover an emergency. Even everyday budgeting can be a losing game when there isn't enough money to cover all the bills. If someone doesn't pay a phone or energy bill on time, they'll get a late fee added onto their next bill, and those fees add up quickly.

Shopping is more expensive, too. Someone living "paycheck to paycheck" (that is, someone who doesn't earn enough money to be able to save anything after all the bills are paid) might only be able to buy the groceries they need for that week or that day. Next time you're in a grocery store, compare the unit price on a small box of cereal and a "family size" box of the same cereal. The larger size is usually more costly overall but cheaper per ounce.

The high cost of poverty can be thought of as an unofficial "poor tax."[95] If someone can't afford to buy a washer and dryer, they'll spend more money going to the laundromat over the long run. If they can't afford regular medical care, they might have to deal with expensive health problems later on. We've talked a lot about making choices with money in this book, but for some of us, there simply isn't a choice.

LEVELING THE PLAYING FIELD

Building wealth through owning a home and having a well-paid job has grown harder. Making the right choices with money is tough when everything seems stacked against you. This isn't to say that people shouldn't try to get good jobs and make smart choices with money. Personal responsibility is important, but good choices don't necessarily make up for the kind of enormous economic changes we've seen in the last few decades.

It is still possible to get a good job without going to college, but there aren't as many of those jobs around as there were when your grandparents and your great-grandparents were younger.[96] Many of these well-paying jobs were in manufacturing: In 1979, there were nearly 20 million manufacturing jobs in the United States, but the global economy has changed drastically in the last fifty years. Now many of the things we use in our daily lives are made in other countries, partly because it's cheaper to run factories in places like Mexico and China. By 2019, the United States had fewer than 13 million manufacturing jobs[97] (and the population grew in that time!).

Global trade has raised the standard of living in countries around the world, and we can now buy many good-quality things for less. But overseas factories have also brought pollution and dangerous working conditions, and fewer people in this country can earn a living making things. Like all our economic choices, trade comes with trade-offs.

Jobs have changed in other ways, too. Computers and automation have cut down on the number of workers needed to do jobs that used to require special skills. These skilled, middle-income jobs disappeared, but they weren't replaced with jobs that paid as well. Instead, job seekers without college degrees took on lower-paying jobs that couldn't easily be done by machines. These are mostly service jobs in places like restaurants, stores, and nursing homes. Like the gig work we talked about in chapter 3, these low-paying jobs often don't come with benefits or regular hours, making it hard to have a predictable income.

They also can't make up for historical forces that led to the strong connection between inequality and race. In 2016, white families in the United States had an average of ten times the wealth of Black families.[98] Black families are twice as likely as white families to live below the poverty line,[99] and even when Black Americans are college educated and own homes, they are more likely to be in debt and less likely to see the value of their home rise.[100] This is due to the history of slavery, the Jim Crow laws that legalized discrimination after slavery was outlawed, and the continuing existence of structural racism.

Societal problems need societal answers. Not everyone agrees on what those answers should be, but here are a few things that have been suggested.

Some countries have a strong economic safety net for their citizens. In Nordic countries like Sweden and Denmark, citizens pay high taxes, and in return, the government provides generous health care, childcare, and retirement programs for everyone. These polices also support a flexible economy, where companies can automate and hire fewer employees without putting those former workers into poverty.[101]

Universal basic income (UBI) programs offer a regular cash payment for everyone. UBI programs don't depend on how much money someone already makes; everyone gets the payment. The money can be spent on anything, unlike other social programs that offer help paying for specific things like groceries or heating bills. UBI is also different from traditional social programs because giving money to everyone takes away the stigma of needing financial help.

Supporters of UBI are looking at the trends we mentioned previously that are making jobs less secure. They're also looking to the future, as the climate changes and, with it, the global economy. Critics of UBI worry that having a guaranteed income will make people less likely to work, but in experiments across the globe, this doesn't seem to be a problem. When the Eastern Band of Cherokee Indians in North Carolina started giving out between $4,000 and $6,000 of casino profits to each tribal member, education levels and mental health improved, and addiction and crime rates went down.[102]

NO FAIR!

We've seen what inequality looks like, but what's wrong with someone having a lot more money than someone else?

In chapter 2, we learned that markets aren't naturally fair. There's no rule in a market system that says that everyone should make the same amount of money or have the same stuff. There's not even a rule that says that everyone should have a decent place to live or enough food to eat.

Some economists argue that inequality is just part of our capitalist system: As the economy grows, some people (the ones who already had investments, owned homes, and owned or managed large companies) are going to benefit more than others, but everyone will benefit in the end. A rising tide lifts all boats, the saying goes. But as we've seen, that hasn't been happening lately. Some boats are getting lifted, and others are running aground.

The problem with inequality isn't just about fairness. We don't all need to earn exactly the same amount of money. After all, we do different kinds of work. We have different skills and different needs. But is it fair for some people to be allowed to have so much more than others? As historian

Matthew Stewart put it, the real problem of inequality is that "some people earn much more than they are worth and most people are worth much more than they earn."[103] Stewart is saying that we all have worth as human beings, and that has nothing to do with how much money we have.

But we're not just looking at individuals and the money they make: We're looking at the system as a whole. Economic inequality (who has the money) is related to social inequality (who has the power). Wealthy people and the industries they work in have a lot more political influence than people who don't have as much money. This means that they can push for laws and regulations that help them get more money or hold on to more of what they already have.

Research also shows that wealth can make people less compassionate toward others.[104] The wealthy who live in wealthy neighborhoods and primarily meet other wealthy people tend to donate less money to charity than wealthy people who live in less-well-off neighborhoods.[105] In one study, drivers of luxury cars were less likely to stop for pedestrians![106]

One of the main problems with the divide between the wealthy and everyone else is that it can lead to a smaller pot for funding all those public goods we talked about. Taxes redistribute money from the well-off to the rest of society, paying for public schools, social programs, and the Social Security payments that go to Americans over the age of sixty-five. These programs help low-income people do better in life. When wealthy people and companies lobby the government to change tax laws, it literally takes possibilities away from everyone else.

If learning about taxes doesn't exactly seem like fun and games, consider this: The board game we call Monopoly was invented by a woman named Elizabeth Magie to teach players about taxes and inequality. Originally, you could play two versions of the game, one that looked like the free-market, cash-grabbing game we know today and one where a land tax redistributed money to all the players instead of rewarding those who were already wealthy.[107] Magie hoped her game would inspire America to create a real-life version of the land tax. If you've ever played Monopoly, where the richest player wins, you know that lesson never stuck. In fact, Magie herself was cheated by a man named Charles Darrow, who claimed to have invented the game himself. Eventually, he sold the game to Parker Brothers, who bought Magie's patent for about $500. That's about as fair as printing your own Get Out of Jail Free cards.

Inequality can sometimes make people on the lower end of the income scale give up trying to get ahead. The high salaries paid to executives are meant to inspire all workers to be productive, but when even incompetent leaders get massive bonuses, other employees might take the opposite message: *I'll never be able to make that kind of money, and if it doesn't matter when someone does a bad job, why should I try my best?* Rising inequality chips away at trust. Just as we need trust to make money itself work, we need to be able to trust in one another to make society work.

Some parents change their behavior in highly unequal societies. In countries where there's a large gap between the rich and the poor, parents in the upper end try to arm their kids against a scary future by controlling more of their time and attention. Send the kids to the best academic summer camps! Keep up with those accordion lessons (or violin or piano)! Insist on perfection! Not all parents act this way, but if you know some who do, it might only be because inequality makes even those who have money worry about their future.[108]

AROUND THE WORLD

This is a lot! And we've mostly talked about the United States. People in the United States are relatively well-off compared to people in many other countries. These days, if we measure inequality around the world, the biggest differences in income and wealth are between different countries, not between people in the same country.[109]

There's a historical reason for that: The United States,

Great Britain, and other countries in the global north benefited enormously from the Industrial Revolution in the eighteenth and nineteenth centuries. Although not everyone gained equally from those changes (no surprise there!), some of the benefits, like public education and better health care, affected most of the population.

In the global south, including countries in Africa, Latin America, and parts of Asia, progress hasn't been as straightforward. The reasons are complicated, and we don't have enough space to do justice to this history, but let's make one connection between these rich and poor countries: The rich countries tend to be those that also benefited from colonization, or taking over a place by force, ruling its people, and taking its wealth. The poorer countries are those that were colonized.[110]

Colonial powers profited by exploiting their colonies' natural resources, like minerals and rubber. They also exploited human beings. In many cases, colonizers enslaved Indigenous and African people to work on their plantations, farms, and other industries. Economic injustice didn't end when countries gained their independence: After fighting the French colonizers to become the world's first Black republic, Haiti was forced to make payments to France to compensate former enslavers! The payments started in 1825, and the debt wasn't fully paid until 1947.[111]

ANOTHER MOON SHOT

Imagine that the richest person in the world isn't the CEO of some tech company. It's you. Through a combination of luck and work, you've made more money than you could ever spend in your life. What are you going to do with it? Mansions? Jets? Swimming pools? Swimming pools on your mansion-size jets? Maybe. Or maybe you decide to visit space.

When you get up there, you look back down at Earth, your tiny blue planet. Suddenly, you're aware of how many people you could help with your money. Are you going to do it by giving it away? By investing it on Earth or starting a space exploration company that will create jobs and possibly colonize Mars? Or are you going to forget all about that and build yourself a more powerful spacecraft so you can race through the stars by yourself? Which of these things would make your life the most meaningful?

We've seen the complicated ways that the story of money gets tied up with the story of human history. We live in a market economy where money brings power. But being human also means we get to make choices that affect the world we live in, whether we're billionaires or not.

CHAPTER SEVEN

How Can We Make Good Choices with Money?

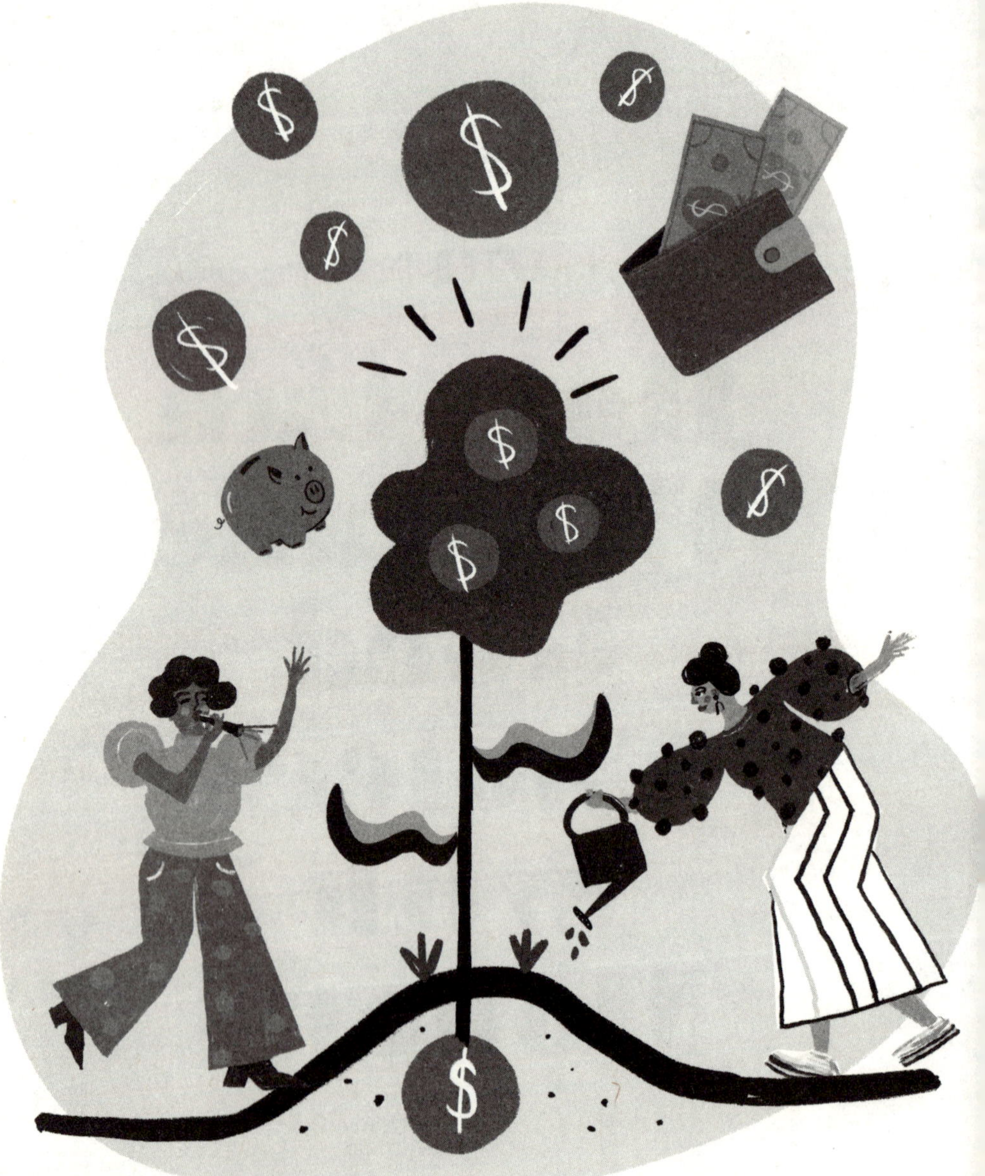

In the future, money might look different than it does now. Maybe none of us will use cash! Or we'll use cryptocurrency or go back to exchanging squirrel pelts. Whatever money will be, you'll need the same skills to use it wisely. Even though money itself might not always be a "real" thing, its effects on people's lives are very real.

This book can't teach you everything you need to know, but with a few basic ideas, you'll be able to find more information in other places when you need it. For our final chapter, let's look at how Present You can start making good choices with money and Future You can keep those good choices going.

MONEY TALKS

None of us are born knowing how to be smart about money. We learn it as we grow up. Some of us learn directly from our families, if they're open to talking about their own values and habits with money. Some of us just pick up on the clues that we see around us by noticing how our families behave and spend. These lessons and clues might be helpful—but they might not! Adults don't all have great habits with money.

For some families, money is an adult problem, not something to share with kids. Adults might feel that thinking too much about money will make you worry about it. Or maybe they think you're not interested. Maybe their families didn't talk to them about money. Or, because they're human (believe it or not), they might feel worried or embarrassed that they don't make as much money as other people.

This kind of secrecy can make people worse off. In general, while American culture pushes consumerism (buying stuff) as a lifestyle and a path to happiness, we're also taught that it isn't polite to talk about money. It's a weird mixed message: *You should be able to afford all this awesome stuff to make your life better, but no one is going to tell you how to afford it! You should keep up with what your friends are buying, but you have no idea how much money their families make or how much money your family makes!*

But here's an undeniable fact: No matter how your family feels and acts around money, you're going to have to use it all your life. The earlier you learn how money works in the real world, the better you'll be at making money choices later on.

If you feel comfortable asking your family or another trusted adult in your life about their money habits and values, go for it. Remember, money questions aren't just about *how much*. The even more important questions are about *how* and *why*.

Here are some questions you can ask:

1. HOW DO YOU MAKE CHOICES ABOUT WHAT TO SAVE AND WHAT TO SPEND? DO YOU MAKE A BUDGET? DO YOU KNOW WHAT YOU SPEND ON DIFFERENT THINGS EVERY MONTH?

2. WHAT DO THINGS COST? HOW MUCH DO YOU PAY FOR RENT OR A HOME LOAN, ELECTRICITY, PHONE AND INTERNET, GROCERIES, AND OTHER BILLS?[112]

3. DO YOU DONATE MONEY TO ORGANIZATIONS THAT YOU SUPPORT? HOW DO YOU DECIDE WHO TO GIVE YOUR MONEY TO AND HOW MUCH TO GIVE?

4. WHAT VALUES AND BELIEFS DO YOU HAVE ABOUT MONEY? HOW IMPORTANT DO YOU THINK IT IS TO SAVE?

5. WHEN YOU'RE TALKING TO SOMEONE WHO IS EMPLOYED: WHAT WAS YOUR FIRST JOB? HOW DID YOU CHOOSE THE JOB YOU HAVE NOW? WHAT TRAINING OR EDUCATION DO YOU NEED TO DO YOUR JOB? HAVE YOU EVER TAKEN ON AN EXTRA JOB TO MAKE ENDS MEET?

6. WHEN DO YOU THINK YOU'LL RETIRE? WHAT DO YOU WANT YOUR LIFE TO BE LIKE WHEN YOU RETIRE?

You can observe how your family behaves with money, too. If your family can afford to make large purchases like cars or vacations, do they research the options first? Or do they make decisions based on a brand name or a recommendation?

Even our small choices reveal something about us. If your family eats in restaurants or gets takeout, do they go for an old favorite every time or try new things? Do they shop at national chain stores, local stores, or both? Or do they buy most of what they need online? Have you ever heard an adult talk about a business they *don't* spend money at because they disagree with the owner's beliefs or actions?

MONEY NOW

Because families have different incomes and different habits and values about money, you might or might not have chances to practice using money now. If you get an allowance, birthday cash, or money for good grades, you can begin there. Same if you have an after-school job walking dogs or shoveling snow. You might get paid in cash, or you might have "real virtual" money in the form of a debit card or cash app.

If you don't have chances to work with real money, you might be able to try it out in the virtual world! Do you play a game that lets you earn virtual gold to spend on tools, pets, accessories, or your virtual house? If games aren't your thing, what about writing or drawing a scenario where you have some cash to spend?

If you have money of your own in any form, and even if you don't, it's time to think about your own money habits and values. There's no one way to do money. Saving is important, but so is enjoying your life, and while many things we enjoy are free, some of them cost money. The goal of being a smart saver isn't that you never, ever spend money. It's that you think carefully about your whole financial picture: How much money do you have, how much do you earn, what do you need to pay for and save for, and how much can you safely spend without making life hard for Future You?

What are some good money habits to practice now? Basically, how to save, how to spend, and how to share.

SAVE, SPEND, SHARE

No matter what kind of money you're working with, a simple and useful way to handle it is to divide it into three categories: save, spend, and share. If you have physical cash, you can use three different containers. If not, you can create the categories on a spreadsheet or in a notebook.

Your Spend account is for buying inexpensive everyday things, like extras in the school cafeteria or gum at the corner store. Your Save account is for larger purchases, things you need to save for over time. And your Share account is for making your own donations to organizations and causes that you believe in.

It's easy to think of things to spend money on. They're all around us: every time you go into a store, every time you see an online ad, every time a friend shows you something they got for their birthday.

When you're trying to decide if you should buy something (say, your very own garden gnome, just for fun), ask yourself a few questions first:

1. WILL I ENJOY THIS GNOME MORE THAN SOMETHING ELSE I COULD SPEND THIS MONEY ON? (IF YOU WANT TO USE YOUR ECONOMICS VOCABULARY, ASK YOURSELF IF THE GNOME WILL PROVIDE YOU WITH MAXIMUM UTILITY.)

2. WOULD I RATHER HAVE THIS GNOME NOW OR SOMETHING ELSE LATER? (THAT'S PRESENT BIAS.)

3. AM I JUST EXCITED ABOUT SPENDING MONEY BECAUSE THE GNOME STORE IS AWESOME AND I'M HANGING OUT WITH FRIENDS? (THAT'S CALLED TRANSACTION UTILITY.)

4. IF I BUY THIS GNOME NOW, HOW MUCH MONEY WILL I HAVE LEFT? HOW LONG WILL IT TAKE ME TO SAVE FOR SOMETHING ELSE?

Enjoyment doesn't always come from spending money on gnomes or anything else, though. You can feel just as good by saving it for a larger purchase or to establish your own bank account. It can also be deeply satisfying to give money to a cause you believe in.

Saving and spending are pretty obvious things to do with money, but why share? If you share your money with others, you'll have less for yourself. Isn't it Present You's job to leave plenty of money for Future You?

Technically, yes. And it's a privilege to have enough money that you can donate some of it. But Future You is also counting on Present You to grow and develop as a member of society and as someone who cares about others.

When we think of charities, we often picture large organizations that feed the hungry or save the polar bears. There's nothing wrong with this kind of giving. But you get to decide where your Share funds go, and they don't have to go to big national charities. There are probably plenty of local organizations that can make even better use of small donations than the big guys can. After all, big charities have people on staff whose job is to go after big donations. Small local groups rely more on the generosity of the people around them who see the good they do in the community.

You might choose to give to a local sports organization that provides equipment and lessons to kids who can't afford to participate in sports. Or you might give to your local animal shelter, library, or volunteer fire department. There's no shortage of ways to use money to do some good in the world!

HOW WILL FUTURE YOU SPEND?

As you get older, you'll have more money to spend, more responsibility, and more complicated choices.

What are the things that affect our choice to buy something or not? Price is a big one: Some of us might have to buy the cheapest option (even if the quality is poor), while those who have more money can afford to spend more now to get something that works better or will last longer.

We might buy something because it was recommended to us by someone we know or because we saw an ad for it featuring our favorite celebrity or a post by a social media influencer. We use our spending power to signal who we are in lots of different ways, from our clothes to our devices to our cars.

Most likely, a good chunk of your income will go to the things you need, like food and housing. Saving something every month for emergencies or toward your retirement is smart, too—it's never too early to think about that! After that, if your budget allows it, you'll have *disposable income*, or money that you can spend on things you want but that aren't basic needs, like gadgets, restaurant meals, or movie tickets. How will your spending reflect who you are?

SAVING

Saving when you're an adult is a little different from saving when you're a kid because you have more tools available to you. Opening up a bank account gives you a tool that no piggy bank can: *compound interest.*

Interest is the small percentage the bank pays you for holding on to your money. Compound interest means that when that percentage is paid, it gets added to the amount of money you have. Then, the next time interest is paid, you get interest on your original investment *plus* on the interest that the bank already paid you!

Say you put $10 into a piggy bank and leave it there for ten years. When you open the piggy bank, you'll still have $10. In a way, you'll have less money than you had when you put it in there because . . . inflation again! Your $10 will be able to buy less stuff because prices were rising while your $10 was sitting in the pig.

Now let's say you put $10 into a high-interest savings account. If the bank pays 3 percent interest compounded monthly, you'll earn 2 or 3 cents a month, and after a year you'll have $10.30. Not impressed? If you put $100 into that account, you'll have $103 after a year. If you put in $1,000, you'll have $1,030, and after five years, you'll have $1,159.27. Five more years and you'd have $1,343.92.

Many savings accounts pay less than 3 percent in interest, but the rate is low because the risk is low, too. The government insures the money you put into a savings account up to $250,000,[113] so if the bank goes out of business, you can still get your money. There are ways to earn a higher return on your money, but they come with higher risk.

The stock market is a little different from a bank account. Unlike a savings account, the stock market doesn't guarantee you a certain interest rate, and your investments aren't insured. On average, the return on stock market investments is about 10 percent.[114] The risk is on you: If you make good investments, your money will grow, but if you make bad investments, you might lose it all! This book isn't telling you where to invest or promising that you'll get rich. However, there are some general rules that smart investors practice: contribute money often, diversify, and think long-term.

Diversification means that instead of putting all your money into a single stock like Clumpy Concrete, you buy shares of a fund that has bundled together a large number of stocks, often for companies in different parts of the economy like technology, health care, and retail. This way, companies that do well will balance out the companies that do poorly. None of us can see into the future to know which companies will fail and which will skyrocket, but diversification is a way to lower the risk of investing.

When you invest, it might be tempting to watch your investments rise and then sell your stock so you can spend that profit. But the power of compounding grows with time: The longer you keep your money in the stock market, the more it will grow! That's something Future You will be very pleased about.

BORROWING

As you get older, you'll have chances not just to earn money but to borrow money. You might take out a college loan or a home loan or get a credit card. Anytime you borrow money to buy something you can't afford today, you agree to pay back the money you borrowed plus interest. That's right—you earn interest when you invest money, and you pay interest when you borrow it! The longer it takes you to pay back a loan, the more you end up paying.

Debt isn't always a bad thing, and it's hard to avoid as

you get older. Being in debt doesn't mean that someone is bad or weak, but it starts to be a problem when you take on debt that (a) you don't really understand, (b) you can't really afford, or (c) you didn't need in the first place.

Credit cards make it almost too easy to spend money you don't have. When Future You gets a credit card, be sure to look at the interest rate and other fees. Then, before you use it, ask yourself the same questions you'd ask yourself now about how much you really want or need whatever it is you're about to buy. If it is something you really need, ask two more questions: How long will it take me to pay this back, and how much will I end up paying overall?

PRIVILEGE

When we talk about what to do with money, we're talking about privilege. Not everyone has enough money to cover their bills; forget about saving and donating. Having money doesn't make you better than someone who doesn't have it, and not having money doesn't make you worse.

If your family makes more money than another family, it's not necessarily because they work harder, and if your family makes less money than another family, it doesn't mean they don't work as hard or don't deserve to live comfortably. How much money you have and what kind of life you live are the result of your family's history and the society you live in, and you can't control that.

One of the unfortunate and ironic things about making good choices with money is that it's usually the people who already have enough of it who have the ability to make the best choices. If you live paycheck to paycheck, setting aside 10 percent of your income for your retirement is impossible.

Studies show that struggling with money takes a mental toll.[115] People with tight budgets have to think much more about getting the best deal when they're shopping. The process of making those small decisions over and over can be exhausting and cause us to think very narrowly about money, leaving low-income people with less time and energy to focus on the bigger picture. It can lead people to make even worse choices than they would if they weren't feeling so stressed out!

MONEY IN THE FUTURE: WORK

What will your typical workday look like when you're an adult? Will you work for a large company or a small non-profit organization? Will you work for yourself? Will you have a day job and do gig work on weekends or evenings, like delivering groceries or driving for a ride-sharing app? You might have an office, or you might work from home, using tools and apps that don't even exist today to connect with your supervisors and your coworkers.

Changes in society and technology mean that the job options you have in ten or twenty years might look different from the jobs you see around you today. We'll probably always need people with certain skills, like doctors, teachers, and plumbers, but the sorts of white-collar office jobs and manufacturing jobs that your grandparents' and parents' generations had will probably look very different.

No matter how the world of work looks when you're an adult, a few habits and skills can help you adapt: collaboration, problem-solving, communication, technology literacy, and, of course, financial literacy.

WHAT ELSE CAN ECONOMICS TEACH US?

Remember that economics isn't always about money. Anytime you have a problem with a scarce resource, you can try thinking like an economist. Say you have a longtime friend who knows that you have several other good friends and feels worried that their friendship isn't important to you.

You might think, *Friendship isn't a scarce resource! I can have lots of friends at the same time, and they're all important to me*. This is absolutely true! But there is a scarce resource in this situation: your time. We're all given the same amount of time, and the way we choose to spend it sends a signal about what we think is valuable. Your friend sees you spending time with other friends and concludes that you find your other friends more valuable.

If you really want to think like an economist, you could open a spreadsheet and start calculating the optimal amount of time to spend with each friend, depending on the activities you enjoy doing together, how close you live to one another, how many other friends they have, and so on. That might end up being more trouble than it's worth!

But recognizing the value of your time and the value your friend places on spending time with you will definitely help you understand your friend's point of view, which is something good friends do. You might also add extra value to your time by doing something fun and special with your friend during your time together.

If you can't calculate an exact amount of time that will bring you and your friend maximum utility, you can always do something else economists love to do: talk!

THE SUM OF EVERYTHING

To sum it all up: Money is important in our lives and in society, but it's not everything. The amount of money you have doesn't say anything about the kind of person you are. As an adult, you'll need to be able to pay your bills and make good choices, but you don't have to be rich to be comfortable and to have a good life.

We live in a complicated economic system that rewards some of us and hurts others. We have to balance our desire for stuff with the limits of the planet we live on. No one can say what your own journey with money will look like, but one thing is for sure: It's never too early to think realistically about your place in the world, your future and the future of others, and what it's going to take for us all to get there.

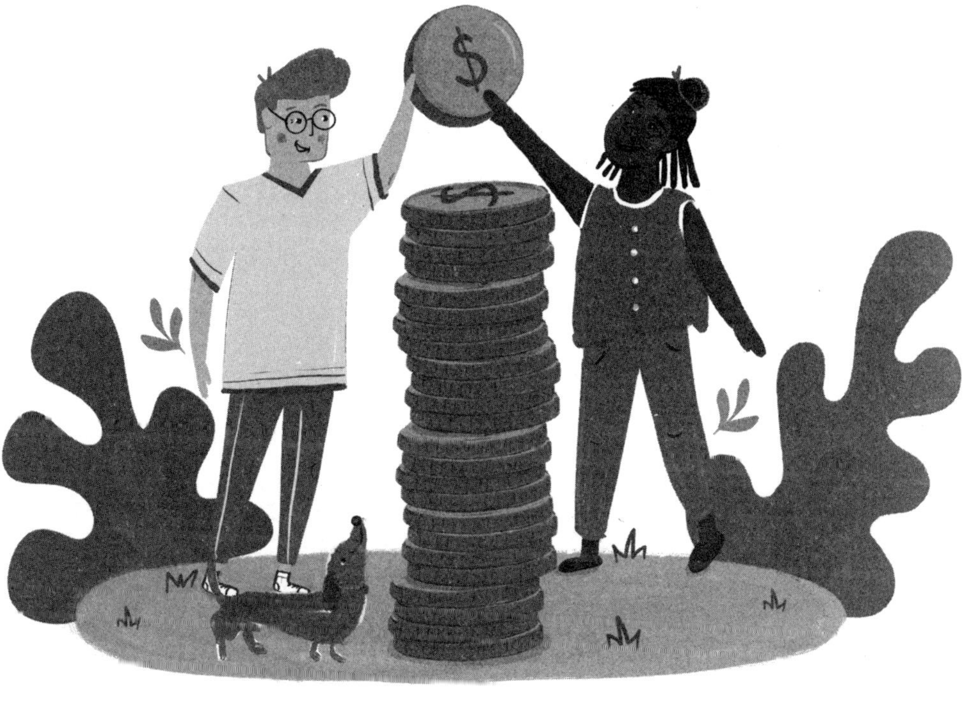

Endnotes

1. David Graeber, *Debt: The First 5,000 Years* (Brooklyn, NY: Melville House, 2011), 30–31.

2. Graeber, *Debt*, 200.

3. "Food and Hunting," Haudenosaunee Confederacy, Accessed May 5, 2023, https://www.haudenosauneeconfederacy.com/historicallife-as-a-haudenosaunee/food-and-hunting/.

4. Graeber, *Debt*, 30.

5. Graeber, *Debt*, 39, 197.

6. Graeber, *Debt*, 197.

7. Graeber, *Debt*, 299.

8. Graeber, *Debt*, 247.

9. Graeber, *Debt*, 205.

10. Jacob Goldstein and Stacy Vanek Smith, "The Invention of Paper Money," *The Indicator from Planet Money*, NPR, September 23, 2020, https://www.npr.org/2020/09/23/916269474/the-invention-of-paper-money.

11. Nobuhiro Kiyotaki and John Moore, "Evil Is the Root of All Money," Clarendon Lectures, London School of Economics, November 26, 2001.

12. Lee C. Cora, "Stone Money of Yap: A Numismatic Survey," *Smithsonian Studies in History and Technology*, 1975, https://repository.si.edu/handle/10088/2422.

13. Robert Michael Poole, "The Tiny Island with Human-Sized Money," BBC Travel, May 3, 2018, https://www.bbc.com/travel/article/20180502-the-tiny-island-with-human-sized-money.

14. Jacob Goldstein and David Kestenbaum, "The Island of Stone Money," *Planet Money*, NPR, December 10, 2010, https://www.npr.org/sections/money/2011/02/15/131934618/the-island-of-stone-money.

15. Jeff Cox, "Cash in Circulation Is Soaring, and That Usually Means Good Things for the Economy," CNBC, January 6, 2021, https://www.cnbc.com/2021/01/05/cash-in-circulation-is-soaring-and-that-usually-means-good-things-for-the-economy.html.

16. "Gross Domestic Product, Fourth Quarter and Year 2021," US Bureau of Economic Analysis, January 27, 2022, https://www.bea.gov/news/2022/gross-domestic-product-fourth-quarter-and-year-2021-advance-estimate.

17. Wayne Duggan and Julie Pinkerton, "The History of Bitcoin, the First Cryptocurrency," *U.S. News and World Report*, May 10, 2023, https://money.usnews.com/investing/articles/the-history-of-bitcoin.

18. Molli Mitchell, "'The Crypto King': What Happened to QuadrigaCX and Is It Still Operating?" *Newsweek*, April 1, 2022, https://www.newsweek.com/what-happened-quadrigacx-bitcoin-operating-gerald-cotten-crypto-king-1694074.

19. Jake Frankenfield, "Cryptocurrency Explained with Pros and Cons for Investment," Investopedia. September 26, 2022, https://www.investopedia.com/terms/c/cryptocurrency.asp.

20. Likos and Hicks, "The History of Bitcoin."

21. Anthony Cuthbertson, "Bitcoin Volatility Hits 2022 Low as Analysts Predict 'Explosive Price Movement,'" Yahoo! Finance, November 4, 2022, https://finance.yahoo.com/news/bitcoin-volatility-hits-2022-low-160840394.html.

22. Thalia Beaty, "Explainer: How Cryptocurrencies Work (and How They Don't)," AP News, April 21, 2022, https://apnews.com/article/cryptocurrency-technology-business-environment-blockchain-0075f9c32e9680c4657890c06a62669b.

23. Nic Carter, "How Much Energy Does Bitcoin Actually Consume?" *Harvard Business Review*, May 5, 2021, https://hbr.org/2021/05/how-much-energy-does-bitcoin-actually-consume.

24. Renee Cho, "Bitcoin's Impacts on Climate and the Environment," *State of the Planet*, Columbia Climate School, September 20, 2021, https://news.climate.columbia.edu/2021/09/20/bitcoins-impacts-on-climate-and-the-environment/.

25. Steven Heller, "Notgeld: Emergency Money in Inflationary Germany," Design Observer, September 26, 2018, https://designobserver.com/feature/notgeld-emergency-money-in-inflationary-germany/39926.

26. Terence Ball, "Communism," Britannica, last modified December 1, 2022, https://www.britannica.com/topic/communism.

27. Dave Blanchard and Kenny Malone, "When Bricks Were Rubles," *Planet Money*, NPR, April 1, 2022. https://www.npr.org/2022/04/01/1090312774/when-bricks-were-rubles.

28. Robert L. Heilbroner, "Economic System," Britannica, https://www.britannica.com/money/topic/economic-system.

29. Charles Wheelan, *Naked Economics* (New York: W. W. Norton, 2010), 65.

30. Julianne Dunn, "COVID-19 and Supply Chains: A Year of Evolving Disruption," Federal Reserve Bank of Cleveland, Accessed February 26, 2021, https://www.clevelandfed.org/events/fedtalk/2021/ft-20210525-covid-19-and-supply-chains-year-of-evolving-disruption.

31. Jaclyn Diaz and Scott Neuman, "'She's Free': Giant Container Ship Blocking Suez Canal Underway after Days," NPR, March 29, 2021, https://www.npr.org/2021/03/29/982174644/ever-given-partially-afloat-as-salvage-teams-race-to-reopen-suez-canal.

32. Mary-Ann Russon, "The Cost of the Suez Canal Blockage," BBC News, March 29, 2021, https://www.bbc.com/news/business-56559073.

33. Karl Vick, "For Charity and Hype, a 'Princess' Beanie," *The Washington Post*, December 24, 1997, https://www.washingtonpost.com/archive/local/1997/12/24/for-charity-and-hype-a-princess-beanie/1d315e11-4869-4728-8a42-9145869c9904/.

34. eBay, March 21, 2022, https://www.ebay.com/b/Princess-Diana-Bear/440/bn_7023351950.

35. Sara Santora, "17 Pounds of Illegal Sperm Whale Vomit Seized by Police in Sting Operation," *Newsweek*, October 26, 2021, https://www.newsweek.com/17-pounds-illegal-sperm-whale-vomit-seized-police-sting-operation-1642795.

36. "Model T," History.com, last modified May 10, 2023, https://www.history.com/topics/inventions/model-t.

37. Jason Fernando, "Inflation: What It Is, How It Can Be Controlled, and Extreme Examples," Investopedia, last modified December 13, 2022, https://www.investopedia.com/terms/i/inflation.asp.

38. Avinash Dixit, *Microeconomics: A Very Short Introduction* (Oxford University Press, 2014), 3.

39. "Fossil Fuels Received $5.9 Trillion in Subsidies in 2020, Report Finds," Yale Environment 360, October 6, 2021, https://e360.yale.edu/digest/fossil-fuels-received-5-99-trillion-in-subsidies-in-2020-report-finds.

40. Brian Resnick and Javier Zarracina, "The U.S. Has a 1.3 Billion-Pound Surplus of Cheese. Let's Try to Visualize That," *Vox*, June 28, 2018, https://www.vox.com/science-and-health/2018/6/28/17515188/us-cheese-surplus-billion-pounds.

41. Monica Anderson et al., "The State of Gig Work in 2021," Pew Research Center, December 8, 2021, https://www.pewresearch.org/internet/2021/12/08/the-state-of-gig-work-in-2021/.

42. Dan Walters, "California's Gig Worker Fight Is Back in the Courts," *CalMatters*, August 25, 2021, https://calmatters.org/commentary/2021/08/californias-gig-worker-fight-is-back-in-the-courts/.

43. Rakesh Kochhar, "The Self-Employed Are Back at Work in Pre-COVID-19 Numbers, but Their Businesses Have Smaller Payrolls," Pew Research Center, November 3, 2021, https://www.pewresearch.org/fact-tank/2021/11/03/the-self-employed-are-back-at-work-in-pre-covid-19-numbers-but-their-businesses-have-smaller-payrolls/.

44. US Bureau of Labor Statistics Reports, "Highlights of Women's Earnings in 2020," September 2021, https://www.bls.gov/opub/reports/womens-earnings/2020/home.htm.

45. Women's Bureau, "Women's Earnings by Race and Ethnicity as a Percentage of White, Non-Hispanic Men's Earnings," US Department of Labor, 2020, https://www.dol.gov/agencies/wb/data/earnings/race-percentage-white-hispanic.

46. Office of the Assistant Secretary for Administration & Management, "Disability Discrimination in the DOL Workplace," US Department of Labor, https://www.dol.gov/agencies/oasam/centers-offices/civil-rights-center/internal/policies/disability-discrimination.

47. U.S. Equal Employment Opportunity Commission, "Jury Awards over $125 Million in EEOC Disability Discrimination Case against Walmart," press release, July 16, 2021, https://www.eeoc.gov/newsroom/jury-awards-over-125-million-eeoc-disability-discrimination-case-against-walmart.

48. Julie Moreau, "'Laughed Out of Interviews': Trans Workers Discuss Job Discrimination," NBC News, October 6, 2019, https://www.nbcnews.com/feature/nbc-out/laughed-out-interviews-trans-workers-discuss-job-discrimination-n1063041.

49. Nina Totenberg, "Supreme Court Delivers Major Victory to LGBTQ Employees," NPR, June 15, 2020, https://www.npr.org/2020/06/15/863498848/supreme-court-delivers-major-victory-to-lgbtq-employees.

50. GMA Team, "House Passes CROWN Act to Ban Discrimination against Race-Based Hairstyles Nationwide," ABC News, March 18, 2022, https://abcnews.go.com/GMA/Style/house-passes-crown-act-ban-discrimination-black-hairstyles/story?id=83528770.

51. Information in this chapter cited from Richard H. Thaler and Cass R. Sunstein, *Nudge: The Final Edition* (New York: Penguin Books, 2021) and Richard Thaler, *Misbehaving: The Making of Behavioral Economics* (New York: W. W. Norton & Company, 2016).

52. Will Wilder, "Voter Suppression in 2020," Brennan Center for Justice, August 20, 2021, https://www.brennancenter.org/our-work/research-reports/voter-suppression-2020.

53. Ehsan Masood, *The Great Invention: The Story of GDP and the Making (and Unmaking) of the Modern World* (New York: Pegasus Books, 2016).

54. "Concrete Needs to Lose Its Colossal Carbon Footprint," editorial, *Nature*, September 28, 2021, https://www.nature.com/articles/d41586-021-02612-5.

55. "Cement: Materials and Manufacturing Process," Greenspec, https://www.greenspec.co.uk/building-design/cement-materials-and-manufacturing-process/.

56. Paul Nelson, "Platteville Limestone," MNopedia, August 10, 2016, https://www.mnopedia.org/thing/platteville-limestone.

57. Vince Beiser, "Sand Mining: The Global Environmental Crisis You've Probably Never Heard Of," *The Guardian*, February 27, 2017, https://www.theguardian.com/cities/2017/feb/27/sand-mining-global-environmental-crisis-never-heard.

58. David C. Holzman, "Accounting for Nature's Benefits: The Dollar Value of Ecosystem Services," *Environmental Health Perspectives* 120, no. 4 (2012): 152–57, https://www.ncbi.nlm.nih.gov/pmc/articles/PMC3339477/.

59. United Nations Climate Change, "Payments for Environmental Services Program: Costa Rica," https://unfccc.int/climate-action/momentum-for-change/financing-for-climate-friendly-investment/payments-for-environmental-services-program.

60. Erin Sills et al., "Impact of Costa Rica's Program of Payments for Environmental Services on Land Use," Latin America and Caribbean Sustainable Development Department, World Bank, October 2008, https://openknowledge.worldbank.org/bitstream/handle/10986/17893/862790NWP0PESL00Box385172B00PUBLIC0.pdf?sequence=1&isAllowed=y.

61. Michael Tobias, "Recycling and Reusing Concrete," Nearby Engineers, November 29, 2019, https://www.ny-engineers.com/blog/recycling-and-reusing-concrete.

62. Nick Romeo, "How Much Do Things Really Cost?" *The New Yorker*, April 2, 2022, https://www.newyorker.com/business/currency/how-much-do-things-really-cost?utm_source=pocket-newtab.

63. The Rockefeller Foundation, "True Cost of Food: Measuring What Matters to Transform the U.S. Food System," Rockefeller Foundation, July 2021, https://www.rockefellerfoundation.org/wp-content/uploads/2021/07/True-Cost-of-Food-Report-Executive-Summary-Final.pdf.

64. "Plastic Water Bottles Made with Advanced Recycling Sold at Target," *Plastics Today*, June 17, 2021, https://www.plasticstoday.com/packaging/plastic-water-bottles-made-advanced-recycling-sold-target.

65. Joe Hernandez, "Accusations of 'Greenwashing' by Big Oil Companies Are Well-Founded, a New Study Finds," NPR, February 16, 2022, https://www.npr.org/2022/02/16/1081119920/greenwashing-oil-companies.

66. European Commission, "Screening of Websites for 'Greenwashing': Half of Green Claims Lack Evidence," press release, January 28, 2021, https://ec.europa.eu/commission/presscorner/detail/en/ip_21_269.

67. "Protecting Spotted Owls Cost Far Fewer Jobs Than Timber Industry Claimed," *UChicago News*, July 8, 2021, https://news.uchicago.edu/story/northern-spotted-owls-conservation-timber-jobs-endangered-species-act.

68. Larry Prusak, "What Can't Be Measured," *Harvard Business Review*, October 7, 2010, https://hbr.org/2010/10/what-cant-be-measured.

69. World Bank, "Population, Total: Bhutan," 2020, https://data.worldbank.org/indicator/SP.POP.TOTL?locations=BT.

70. Karma Ura et al., "A Short Guide to Gross National Happiness Index," The Centre for Bhutan Studies, 2012, https://doi.org/10.35648/20.500.12413/11781/ii025.

71. "Bhutan Is the World's Only Carbon Negative Country, so How Did They Do It?" Climate Council, February 4, 2017, https://www.climatecouncil.org.au/bhutan-is-the-world-s-only-carbon-negative-country-so-how-did-they-do-it/.

72. Jackie Wattles, "Virgin Galactic Founder Richard Branson Successfully Rockets to Outer Space," CNN, July 12, 2021, https://www.cnn.com/2021/07/11/tech/richard-branson-virgin-galactic-space-flight-scn/index.html.

73. Marcia Dunn, "Jeff Bezos Blasts into Space on Own Rocket: 'Best Day Ever!'" AP News, July 20, 2021, https://apnews.com/article/jeff-bezos-space-e0afeaa813ff0bdf23c37fe16fd34265.

74. Alexandra Hutzler, "Jeff Bezos Thanks Amazon Workers, Customers after Space Trip: 'You Guys Paid for All This,'" *Newsweek*, July 20, 2021, https://www.newsweek.com/jeff-bezos-thanks-amazon-workers-customers-after-space-trip-you-guys-paid-all-this-1611557.

75. Tom Huddleston Jr., "Richard Branson vs. Jeff Bezos: How the Two Space-Bound Billionaires Stack Up," CNBC, July 19, 2021, https://www.cnbc.com/2021/07/02/branson-vs-bezos-how-the-two-space-bound-billionaires-stack-up.html.

76. Reuters, "Amazon Hikes Average U.S. Starting Pay to $18, Hires for 125,000 Jobs," *U.S. News & World Report*, September 14, 2021, https://money.usnews.com/investing/news/articles/2021-09-14/exclusive-amazon-hikes-starting-pay-to-18-an-hour-as-it-hires-for-125-000-more-logistics-jobs.

77. Joseph Stiglitz, *The Price of Inequality* (New York: W. W. Norton, 2013), 73.

78. "The American Dream Is Fading," Opportunity Insights, May 5, 2023, https://opportunityinsights.org/national_trends/.

79. Estelle Sommeiller and Mark Price, "The New Gilded Age," Economic Policy Institute, July 19, 2018, https://www.epi.org/publication/the-new-gilded-age-income-inequality-in-the-u-s-by-state-metropolitan-area-and-county/#epi-toc-6.

80. "Distribution of Household Wealth in the U.S. Since 1989," March 24, 2023, Board of Governors of the Federal Reserve System, https://www.federalreserve.gov/releases/z1/dataviz/dfa/distribute/table/.

81. Matthew Stewart, *The 9.9 Percent* (New York: Simon & Schuster, 2022), chapter 1.

82. Douglas Broom, "Inequality Is Not Confined to Humans. Animals Are Divided by Privilege Too," The Print, January 15, 2022, https://theprint.in/featured/inequality-is-not-confined-to-humans-animals-are-divided-by-privilege-too/804179/.

83. "Warren Buffett and His Secretary on Their Tax Rates," ABC News, January 25, 2012, https://abcnews.go.com/blogs/business/2012/01/warren-buffett-and-his-secretary-talk-taxes.

84. Lawrence Mishel and Jori Kandra, "CEO Pay Has Skyrocketed 1,322% since 1978," Economic Policy Institute, August 10, 2021, https://www.epi.org/publication/ceo-pay-in-2020/.

85. Daniel Kurt, "Corporate Leadership by Gender," Investopedia, February 22, 2022, https://www.investopedia.com/corporate-leadership-by-gender-5113708.

86. L. Hunter Lovins et al., *A Finer Future: Creating an Economy in Service to Life* (Gabriola, BC, Canada: New Society Publishers, 2018).

87. Daniel Liberto, "Vulture Capitalist," Investopedia, May 3, 2022, https://www.investopedia.com/terms/v/vulturecapitalist.asp.

88. Jeffrey B. Wenger and Melanie A. Zaber, "Most Americans Consider Themselves Middle-Class. But Are They?" Rand Corporation, May 14, 2021, https://www.rand.org/blog/2021/05/most-americans-consider-themselves-middle-class-but.html.

89. Melanie Hanson, "Average Cost of College by Year," Education Data Initiative, January 9, 2022, https://educationdata.org/average-cost-of-college-by-year.

90. "Trends in Health Care Spending," AMA, https://www.ama-assn.org/about/research/trends-health-care-spending.

91. Emmie Martin, "Here's How Much Housing Prices Have Skyrocketed over the Last 50 Years," CNBC Money, June 23, 2017, https://www.cnbc.com/2017/06/23/how-much-housing-prices-have-risen-since-1940.html.

92. Terry Gross, "As Child Care Costs Soar, Providers Are Barely Getting By," *Fresh Air*, NPR, December 16, 2021, https://www.npr.org/2021/12/16/1064794349/child-care-costs-biden-plan.

93. Drew Desilver, "For Most U.S. Workers, Real Wages Have Barely Budged in Decades," Pew Research Center, August 7, 2018, https://www.pewresearch.org/fact-tank/2018/08/07/for-most-us-workers-real-wages-have-barely-budged-for-decades/.

94. Molly Kinder et al., "With Inflation Surging, Big Companies' Wage Upticks Aren't Nearly Enough," Brookings, December 13, 2021, https://www.brookings.edu/blog/the-avenue/2021/12/13/with-inflation-surging-big-companies-wage-upticks-arent-nearly-enough/.

95. Buzzfeed, "People Are Sharing Examples of 'Unofficial Taxes on the Poor' and It's Accurate as Hell," MSN, April 9, 2022, https://www.msn.com/en-us/money/personalfinance/people-are-sharing-examples-of-unofficial-taxes-on-the-poor-and-it-s-accurate-as-hell/ar-AAW2KZU.

96. David Autor, "The Shrinking Share of Middle-Income Jobs," Econofact, March 14, 2022, https://econofact.org/the-shrinking-share-of-middle-income-jobs.

97. Katelynn Harris, "Forty Years of Falling Manufacturing Employment," *Beyond the Numbers: Employment and Unemployment* 9, no. 16, U.S. Bureau of Labor Statistics (November 2020), https://www.bls.gov/opub/btn/volume-9/forty-years-of-falling-manufacturing-employment.htm.

98. Dorothy A. Brown, *The Whiteness of Wealth: How the Tax System Impoverishes Black Americans and How We Can Fix It* (New York: Crown, 2021), 28.

99. Kyle K. Moore, "The Case for Stratification Economics," *The Black Agenda: Bold Solutions for a Broken System*, ed. Anna Gifty Opoku-Agyeman (New York: St. Martin's Press, 2022).

100. Brown, *The Whiteness of Wealth*, 117.

101. James McWhinney, "The Nordic Model: Pros and Cons," Investopedia, January 26, 2022, https://www.investopedia.com/articles/investing/100714/nordic-model-pros-and-cons.asp.

102. Sigal Samuel, "Everywhere Basic Income Has Been Tried, in One Map," *Vox*, October 20, 2020, https://www.vox.com/future-perfect/2020/2/19/21112570/universal-basic-income-ubi-map.

103. Stewart, *The 9.9 Percent*, 31.

104. Daisy Grewel, "How Wealth Reduces Compassion," *Scientific American*, April 10, 2012, https://www.scientificamerican.com/article/how-wealth-reduces-compassion/.

105. "Who Gives Most to Charity?" Philanthropy Roundtable, January 20, 2023, https://www.philanthropyroundtable.org/resource/who-gives-most-to-charity/.

106. University of Nevada, Las Vegas, "Drivers of Expensive Cars Less Likely to Yield for Pedestrians," *Science Daily*, February 26, 2020, https://www.sciencedaily.com/releases/2020/02/200226171110.htm.

107. Roman Mars, "The Landlord's Game," *99% Invisible* (transcript), November 17, 2015, https://99percentinvisible.org/episode/the-landlords-game/transcript/.

108. Stewart, *The 9.9 Percent*, chapter 2.

109. Angus Deaton, *The Great Escape: Health, Wealth, and the Origins of Inequality* (Princeton, NJ: Princeton University Press, 2013), 183.

110. James Robinson and Darren Acemoğlu, "The Economic Impact of Colonialism," *VoxEU*, January 30, 2017, https://voxeu.org/article/economic-impact-colonialism.

111. Dan Sperling, "In 1825, Haiti Paid France $21 Billion to Preserve Its Independence—Time for France to Pay It Back," *Forbes*, December 6, 2017, https://www.forbes.com/sites/realspin/2017/12/06/in-1825-haiti-gained-independence-from-france-for-21-billion-its-time-for-france-to-pay-it-back/?sh=2c11d674312b.

112. These prices will likely rise between now and the time you're paying your own bills (hello, inflation), but if an adult is willing to share this information with you, learning what things cost now will help you see the full picture of an adult's or family's financial life.

113. Alexandria White, "How FDIC Insurance Works, Plus a Breakdown of Coverage Limits," CNBC, October 23, 2020, https://www.cnbc.com/select/fdic-insurance/.

114. J. B. Maverick, "S&P 500 Average Return," Investopedia, January 13, 2022, https://www.investopedia.com/ask/answers/042415/what-average-annual-return-sp-500.asp.

115. Stiglitz, *The Price of Inequality*, 142.